STRAIGHT

THE **SUNY** SERIES

CULTURAL STUDIES IN CINEMA/VIDEO

WHEELER WINSTON DIXON | EDITOR

STRAIGHT

❈

Constructions of Heterosexuality in the Cinema

WHEELER
WINSTON
DIXON

STATE UNIVERSITY OF NEW YORK PRESS

Published by
State University of New York Press, Albany

© 2003 State University of New York

For information, address State University of New York Press,
90 State Street, Suite 700, Albany, NY 12207

Production by Marilyn P. Semerad
Marketing by Patrick Durocher

Library of Congress Cataloging-in-Publication Data

Dixon, Wheeler W., 1950–
    Straight : constructions of heterosexuality in the cinema / Wheeler Winston Dixon.
       p. cm. — (The SUNY series, cultural studies in cinema/video)
    Includes bibliographical references and index.
    ISBN 0-7914-5623-4 (alk. paper) — ISBN 0-7914-5624-2 (pbk. : alk. paper)
       1. Man-woman relationships in motion pictures. 2. Sex role in motion pictures. 3.
Masculinity in motion pictures. I. Title. II. Series.

PN1995.9.M27 D59 2003
791.43'63538—dc21

                                                                      2002030447

10 9 8 7 6 5 4 3 2 1

For Gwendolyn

Nothing is so firmly believed as what we least know.

—Montaigne (1533–1592),
Book i, Chap. xxxi,
Of Divine Ordinances

CONTENTS

ILLUSTRATIONS

ACKNOWLEDGMENTS

Brief portions of this text originally appeared in the following publications: "Robert Downey, Sr.: The Preston Sturges of the 1960s," *Popular Culture Review* 13.1 (Jan. 2002); and "British Film Comedy in the New Millennium: Rik Mayall, Adrian Edmondson, and *Guest House Paradiso,*" *Popular Culture Review* 12.1 (Feb. 2001): my thanks to Felicia Campbell, editor. "No More Excuses: An Interview with Robert Downey Sr.," and "An Interview with Jamie Babbit," *Post Script* 21.1 (Fall, 2001); my thanks to Gerald Duchovnay, editor. My sincerest thanks, as always, to Dana Miller, for her expertise and patience in typing this manuscript; and to Kathryn Koldehoff, for her meticulous assistance in the final preparation of the text.

INTRODUCTION

"Play straight with me." "Get straight." "You better go straight." "Straighten up." "That's not straight." "Follow the straight path." "Speak straight." "I vote the straight Republican ticket." *The American Heritage College Dictionary* defines *straight* as, among other things, "right, correct, . . . not deviating from the socially normal, usual, or acceptable . . . conventional to an extreme degree . . . heterosexual . . . [and] honest, law-abiding, or virtuous" ("Straight"). In the sense that it does not deviate in its portrayal of that which is considered "normal," practically all mainstream cinema is straight, and has been since cinema's inception. All video games are straight, as are most books; when something is not straight, it is marked with a special label and is commodified in a different manner than "straight" commercial merchandise. All societal mass communication is heterosexually privileged; the arbiters of public discourse assume that they are speaking to a straight audience. Thus straightness becomes the normative system of values for the dominant social discourse, just as whiteness is seen as the "majority" and all other ethnicities make up the "minorities." But just like whiteness, straightness is a construct, something that doesn't really exist, a concept that needs constant reaffirmation to keep it from disappearing.

Every other mode of social discourse is "other," whether it be termed *gay* (or the newly acceptable *queer*), *bisexual*, or *asexual*, or embodied in the concept of the *spinster*, the *confirmed bachelor*, the *old maid*, or the *same-sex couple* who will never fit into the "straight" world, and doesn't or don't want to. The state of nonstraightness is essentially suspect; it is not seen as "right [or] correct." It is something different, something to be carefully examined and, if at all possible, avoided. That which is not straight is seen as something that is not part of the supposedly normative system of values, something that is a potential threat to the family, to the dominant social system, something that needs to be erased. Almost all films end up with the suture or closure of a marriage or a coupling; indeed, the recent rash of Julia Roberts films demonstrates that Americans (and other members of the American cinema colonies) are more smitten than ever with the idea of the ideal, heterotopic couple, the safe haven of normative romance.

Marriage and heterosexual coupling are seen as the normative values, to be trifled with at one's peril. Married couples are privileged, both socially (they get invited out as a safe social unit because they are yoked to each other) and financially (income taxes aside, spouses get breaks on health insurance, car insurance, schooling, and other expenses). Both members of the married unit need not hold down jobs; to many, in fact, it is better if the woman stays home and stays out of the workplace. Her husband's benefits will cover her; she is the keeper of the domestic hearth above all else. There is a great nostalgia for couplehood and marriage, as exemplified by the Eisenhower-era marriage of George W. and Laura Bush, as opposed to the independent and "threatening" behavior of Geraldine Ferraro, Hillary Clinton, Bella Abzug, and other women in political life.

Consumption too is tied in with straightness: the happy heterosexual couple goes camping, goes boating, goes to a restaurant, washes a car, fixes up a house—all complete with children in the background, as totemic proof of the heteroperformativity of their union. People who do not have children are routinely described as "childless" (rather than "child free"): there must be something wrong, people assume, with their union. To those who are not straight, the social license given to straight people is obvious. In most cities and states within the United States, an attempt by a nonstraight person to buy a greeting card or life insurance for their partner, or to find health insurance, met with a sharp rebuff.

However, propositions such as Nebraska's Defense of Marriage referendum (Initiative 416) signal clearly that, for all its supposed ubiquity and uniformity, marriage and coupling are destabilized—and unstable—concepts. Initiative 416 passed, while 30 percent of the voters cast their ballots against the amendment, which specifically disallows all non-heterosexual partnerships.

Nebraska's Defense of Marriage Amendment would deny basic family rights to gay and lesbian couples. . . . Harvard-educated lawyer Evan Wolfson said the initiative would deny a gay or lesbian family counseling in a domestic abuse case and even the right to say goodbye to his or her partner in the hospital. "It is intended only to attack the family relationships between lesbian and gay Nebraskans," Wolfson said. (Kauffman)

In Vermont, the voters rejected a similar bill, though not without a serious backlash from those who see heterosexual coupling as the only possible model for life partnership. When voters rejected the Vermont bill, a furious political action committee (PAC) struck back with a ringing denunciation of the action, written under the rubric of "Restoring Traditional Vermont Values," on their home page. The PAC's aim, according to its mission statement, was to

[r]epeal "gay marriage" by raising and spending money on mission critical election projects, using professional vendors, in the last two weeks before the September Primary and November General Election. Fund projects, which if funded adequately, will seriously enhance grassroot [sic] volunteer efforts to repeal Vermont's new gay marriage law called "Civil Union" by electing a Pro-Marriage governor and the needed Pro-Marriage legislators. (Vermont)

So it seems that the heterocentric concept of marriage is indeed under attack. Why else would it need "defense"? Americans are instinctively threatened by those who are deemed "not one of us," "not part of the crowd." Consider the popular, all-purpose epithet, "that's different," which implies that whatever person or behavior is under consideration is definitely not part of the straight normative values that Middle America sees as its birthright. Unlike people in Holland, Belgium, Sweden, and other more enlightened countries long ago learned to embrace the concept of difference; unlike them, American society is frightened of difference and seeks to enforce an artificial homogeneity upon all of its citizens, whether they wish to subscribe to these notions of socialized behavior or not.

Hollywood cinema is the dominant cinema of the world, America's single most influential and important cultural industry, with mainstream films now earning more overseas than they do domestically. In Hollywood cinema, these values are reinforced and inculcated in each new generation of cinemagoers as part of the overall social fabric of the moviegoing experience. Films that do not partake of "straight" culture get marginal releases, unless they present sexual difference itself as an untenable and unstable concept, as in such films as *The Crying Game* (1992) and *Hedwig and the Angry Inch* (2000). These films present transgendered individuals as freaks and novelties, and exploit the difference of their transgendered and/or homosexual characters rather than celebrate it or simply state it as a matter of fact. Anything that is not heterosexual, or "straight," is not normative; it is different, suspect, open to immediate investigation, marginalization, and social suspicion.

Straight *couples* are the best consumers, after all: they need houses; they have children, who need clothing and food; they need minivans and sport utility vehicles, which need gasoline, air filters, and tires; they need toys, vacations, anniversary celebrations, and additions to their existing homes when new children arrive. Corporate America is much better off financially targeting these common integers of the dominant social discourse; they'll make more money doing it. When couples overextend themselves, they need loans at usurious rates; they need to mortgage the homes in which they house their children and possessions and reduce all their outstanding bills to "one low monthly payment," a payment that they must nevertheless faithfully meet or they will lose all they possess. And part of what the heterosexual nuclear family possesses, of course, is a place in the dominant society; when a family defaults on a home improvement loan or a bill consolidation loan, they become homeless and enter a demimonde of society where no one but those in "faith-based" charities will care for them. So, Hollywood says, if you don't belong in this film—for whatever reason—get the hell out, because there are thousands crossing the borders each day who would love to take your privileged place.

By constantly reifying the dream of heterotopia, Hollywood hopes to urge us to consume more, more, and still more, so that there will always be a marketplace to serve. Is it any wonder that contemporary feature film directors come straight to the cinema from making television commercials or music videos (which are essentially ads for the performers they contain)? Just like a quart of milk or a pound of hamburger, films all have a "sell by" date; they must perform in the marketplace immediately and find their niche, or perish. This is why five million dollars were spent on the premiere of *Pearl Harbor* (2001). A film must immediately find a foothold at the box office and crush its competition to dominate the marketplace. Even such aggressive marketing tactics do not in and of themselves guarantee an audience; *Pearl Harbor* was edited and repackaged for foreign consumption in Germany and Japan, where the film must do well for the producers to recoup their investment. For all the ballyhoo, the film did only middling business and, in view of its immense cost, is nowhere near breaking even as it crossed the $200 million mark in domestic rentals. Yet, as I'll discuss, what the producers really hoped to sell with *Pearl Harbor* was a love story, not a war story—a love story that would once again restate the values of heteroperformative behavior so zealously reinforced by the dominant cinema.

Indeed, straight heterocentric performativity is now the national model, as mandated by HR 3396. HR 3396 makes male-female marriages the only type of partnership legally recognized throughout the United States. Calling the enactment of the legislation "a deplorable act of hostility," the American Civil Liberties Union (ACLU) noted that the measure

> would deny federal recognition of marriages between lesbian and gay couples. In addition to redefining the Federal definition of marriage, the bill would create a "gay exception" to the Constitution's Full Faith and Credit Clause by allowing states to ignore same-sex marriages performed in any other state. The House vote in favor of the bill was 342 to 67; the Senate approved it by a vote of 84 to 15. President Clinton signed the legislation. (American Civil Liberties Union)

The bill, which was first introduced on 7 May 1996, had two aims and paved the way for the state-by-state battle currently underway. As summarized by one legal authority, "[t]he Defense of Marriage Act (DOMA) does two things. First, it provides that no State shall be required to give effect to a law of any other State with respect to a same-sex 'marriage.' Second, it defines the words 'marriage' and 'spouse' for purposes of Federal law" ("'Defense'"). The actual language of the bill in these matters is direct and unambiguous. In its definition of *marriage* and *spouse,* the act states,

> In determining the meaning of any Act of Congress, or of any ruling, regulation, or interpretation of the various administrative bureaus and agencies of the United States, the word "marriage" means only a legal union between one man and one woman as husband and wife, and the word "spouse" refers only to a person of the opposite sex who is a husband or a wife. ("'Defense'")

Thus, since this act was signed, all gay couples have been excluded from the American social system and relegated automatically to second-class status. The bill, in part, denies gay couples

> bereavement or sick leave to take care [of] a partner or a partner's child; pension or social security continuation when a partner dies; the ability to keep a jointly owned home if a partner goes on Medicaid, dies, or becomes sick; joint tax returns and exemptions for primary relationships on estate taxes; veteran's discounts on medical care, education, and home loans; [and] immigration and residency for partners from other countries. (Partners)

All of this is done in the name of "upholding" supposedly normative values. If this were not enough, Congress is currently considering a wider ban on same-sex marriages, one that the Bush White House will no doubt enthusiastically embrace. The outpouring of rage against the idea of allowing same-sex partnerships equal access under the law has resulted in numerous editorials in the right-wing press attacking the so-called homosexual lobby for pushing their agenda on the public as a whole. But isn't it the other way around? No "homosexual lobby" is telling anyone whom they should desire or what lifestyle they should pursue; it remains a matter of individual choice. Yet straight America wants to set the rules by which human sexuality itself can be regulated, and if at least 10 percent of the population is marginalized as they pursue this goal, they feel, so be it.

At the same time, the outpouring of rage against the idea of same-sex partnerships reveals the fear with which straight Americans regard the notion of same-sex relationships. Not only is everyone in American society assumed to be straight: being straight is, as in the dictionary, equated with decency, and any deviance from the regime of straightness is thus highly undesirable. Hollywood assumes that everyone in society is straight and that the ideal audience for Hollywood films is the heterotopic couple (and so it also considers itself as reflecting dominant normative values). Public schools are designed for straight kids; gay and lesbian kids attend at their peril, and are the subjects of constant ridicule and abuse. Hospitals are designed for straight people: when visiting patients, doctors and nurses routinely ask, "Are you family?" They are implying a heterosexual union. The police are supposed to be straight and are required to uphold straight values; when police officers within the force "come out," they are subject to ritual abuse and potentially the loss of their jobs. Firemen are assumed to be straight; the laws of the United States with regard to property, inheritance, and taxes are designed for straights; banks cater to straight people with "couples discounts"; ad agencies try to sell shampoo, cars, clothing, food, dishwashers, floor cleansers, furniture, dog food, lamps, rugs, cereal, and candy bars to straights.

Television and film overwhelmingly cater to straights, with the exception of artificially whimsical characters on such shows as *Will & Grace*. There being gay is seen as a kooky, aberrant form of behavior existing within a dominant world of incessant heterosexual coupling. Photographers and videographers cater to straights with wedding videos and staged photo albums, to say nothing of the endless photo ops that children provide. Most important, perhaps, straights may routinely display affection for one another on public streets, with a kiss on the cheek or mouth, when such a display between two same-sex partners might well be the excuse for yet another round of gay and/or lesbian bashing. In short, straights may perform their sexual desire in public, but gays and lesbians may not. Thus societal space is safe for straights, dangerous for lesbians and gays. Straights may hold hands, but lesbians and gays run a decided social risk if they do so. Straights are encouraged to share bank accounts and homes, as well as to leave money and living wills with one another.

Straights are allowed to hug. Macho men can get away with hugs in the aftermath of a sports event, and straight women chastely embrace in greeting or in a perfunctory gesture of sympathy without societal comment, but gays are prohibited from displaying such emotions. Straights get tables in restaurants as couples without argument, and they are offered "family meals" and "family buffets," as if the only family that could possibly exist is a straight family. Indeed, "family values" takes its name from the very construct of the straight nuclear family: a husband, a wife, and two kids. It comes as a shock to much of America that queers can create families; bisexuals can create families; nonsexual straights can make up families; transgendered people can constitute families; even members of a group possessing different sexual orientations can constitute a family, although this situation is seldom presented on the screen (one rare example that comes to mind is *Tell Me That You Love Me, Junie Moon* [1970], in which a gay man in a wheelchair, a horribly scarred young woman, and a young man facing death from a terminal illness gather together to create for themselves a home and family, much to society's disapproval).

Straights, of course, can expect to walk down the streets and not be "straight bashed"; straights can strike up conversations with potential partners in bars without, in most cases, risking bodily harm or even death. Straight couples can stay together in hotel rooms without causing comment; straight couples who share a house do not elicit the same suspicion that two men or two women who share a home often do. Straight people enjoy pretty much the same privileges that white people do, but straight whites enjoy even more immunity from social disapproval. Within the mainstream cinema, there are always elements within a film's narrative line that question the supremacy of straightness and the perks that go with it. However, these figures usually operate at the margins of a film's narrative, as Greg Kinnear's character does in *As Good As It Gets* (1997). And naturally, Kinnear's character eventually becomes the victim of gay bashing and thus becomes an object of pity rather than a serious character. In the justly infamous *Pretty Woman* (1990), even the relationship between a prostitute and her john is accorded the status of a heterotopic love affair.

Performing straightness entails rigid self-discipline. It is a state of monotony, repetition, and predictability. It enshrines those who compete in violent sports as heroes, while it marginalizes those who write books other than thrillers or romances(the books one can find in any airport in the world). Straight people play golf, aspire to be upwardly mobile, and are never satisfied with the material possessions they have; they always want more, and they feel that they are entitled to more by their sexual orientation and corporeal self-government. Straight women must be interested in children and must obey the call to become mothers, a call that is endlessly celebrated in mainstream cinema. They must return the gazes of men with appreciation and availability; they must make allowances for the behavioral quirks of their masculine opposites, mothering them, encouraging them, and providing sexual satisfaction on demand. Straightness is work. Straightness wears a tie or a dress. Men must have deep voices, must not be interested in art, cooking, music, sewing, or reading, all seen as traditionally feminine pursuits. Straight men must always make aggressive and suggestive comments to and/or about women, who are expected to view this attention as both expected and desired. Straight men objectify women; straight women expect them to do it.

Straight women, for their part, must be ashamed of their own sexuality and attractiveness, using it only for procreation and not for pleasure, but they must at all costs maintain their availability and present themselves to the world in a highly ritualized form of body display: "I'm

putting on my face." Straight women aren't supposed to be bold or seductive, unless it's in a porn film; or in a noir film, in which case they will be
punished for their sexual aggression; or in an action film, in which case
they may fight another woman and occasionally even a man—in self-
defense—but, ultimately, they must allow themselves to be extricated
from real danger by the film's putative hero. Straight girls must giggle and
use high voices. Straight boys may not express interest in straight girls
until puberty, and then only in a highly prescribed fashion, reinforced by
school dances, parking lot make-out sessions, and family celebrations.
Only "bad" straight girls and women embrace their sexuality; "good"
straight women repress their carnal desires. Straight girls and women
must prefer to socialize exclusively with other straight females; the same
holds true of their male counterparts. Straight couples must bond with
other straight couples to survive within the community; they must be soc-
cer moms and football coaches, and cook up a mean barbecue. Anyone
else is an outsider.

"Old maids" are seen as barren and pitiful. In films and television,
when older women do talk about sex it is usually for comic relief, or it is
presented as nostalgia for their heterosexual past. The same holds true for
old bachelors, but men are allowed to go fishing. Both sets of seniors are
welcome on all-inclusive cruise ships, as Jack Lemmon, Walter Matthau,
and Donald O'Connor proved in the geriatric comedy *Out to Sea* (1997).
When they exhibit sexual interest, they star in *Grumpy Old Men* (1993)
or *Grumpier Old Men* (1995). When older men express heterosexual
desire in these films, as the late Burgess Meredith did in both films, it is
routinely played for comedy.

It would be impossible to write about all the straight film texts in the
cinematic universe, and I have no intention of doing so in this book. In my
selection of texts for analysis, I have included some well-known genres and
some that are not as well recognized, as well as some famous personages,
along with others who have exerted considerable sociosexual influence at
the edges of mainstream cinema, critiquing the very medium in which they
ostensibly participate. Thus this book is a de-centered text, not one that
seeks the artificial safety of a phantom zone of known heteroperformative
desire. I discuss the concept of straightness as it operates at the margins of
cinematic discourse rather than deal with such obvious examples as John
Wayne, Clint Eastwood, Humphrey Bogart, Arnold Schwarzenegger, and
Jean-Claude Van Damme as heterosexualized performative males, and with

such obvious examples as Demi Moore, Julia Roberts, Jennifer Lopez, Dolly Parton, Angelina Jolie, and Sandra Bullock as stereotypical hypersexualized, performative females. Although I do mention these figures in passing. I assume that the reader is well aware of their filmic exploits.

Rather, in this book, I seek to align myself with those persons who question the overriding concept of heteroperformativity in the main-stream cinema, those who, as actors, writers, or directors, have created visions of the heterotopic dream as imperfect. Early on, Thomas Edison, Georges Méliès, and other early cineastes exploited the human body and idealized the heterosexual performative model as the dominant mode of cinematic social discourse. Films by Alice Guy Blaché and others con-tested this model. In the 1950s, during a period of intense social repres-sion, the late Jim Thompson created a brutal series of paperback novels that caught the American imagination. Thompson is the author of the screenplays or novels for the films *Hit Me* (1996), *The Getaway* (1994 and 1972), *The Grifters* (1990), *After Dark, My Sweet* (1990), *The Kill-Off* (1989), *Coup de torchon* (1981), *Série noire* (1979), *The Killer Inside Me* (1976), and other works (including collaborations with Stanley Kubrick).

In Thompson's world, husbands and wives don't necessarily get along; indeed, at times they want to kill each other. In *This World, Then the Fire-works* (which was made into a memorable film in 1997 with Billy Zane and Gina Gershon), Chicago newspaper reporter Marty Lakewood (Zane) is on the run from the cops, whom he has implicated in his news-paper column in numerous scandals. Marty seeks refuge in his California hometown with his slatternly mother (Rue McClanahan) and his prosti-tute sister, Carol (Gina Gershon), with whom Marty is having an inces-tuous affair. This is presented in a matter-of-fact manner, as if the arrangement and relationship of the characters is nothing unusual, or even particularly sordid. Thompson's work, discussed later, became the basis of a neo-noir revival when the original noir model was finally exhausted through repetition.

The *Carry On* comedy films were immensely popular in both Britain and the United States upon their initial release and have today developed a cult following comparable to that of the teleseries *The Avengers* and *Dr. Who*. In them, performative heterosexuality is relentlessly spoofed by such regulars as Sid James (as the eternally lecherous seducer), Barbara Wind-sor (as the bubbly blond who is ever the object of his attentions), and Kenneth Williams (an openly gay man in a period when it was exceedingly difficult to openly admit, even in the most liberal circles, that one was not a heterosexual). In the brutal knockabout comedies of Adrian Edmondson and Rik Mayall (such as their numerous television programs and their first feature film, *Guest House Paradiso* [1999]), we find two heterosexualized males who continually ridicule the concept of enforced heteroperformativity, not only in their own behavior but in the rigidly enforced heterotopia of the Nice family, a husband-and-wife-with-two-children unit who are unfortunate enough to stay in the pair's rundown hotel. Director Robert Downey offers brutal commentaries on conventional heterosexualized behavior, especially in his groundbreaking films *Putney Swope* (1969) and *Chafed Elbows* (1966).

The location of the classical Hollywood western, Old Tucson, served as a home for the films of John Wayne, William Holden, Barbara Stanwyck, Jean Arthur, Robert Mitchum, Dean Martin, Jack Elam, and a host of other heteroperformative western genre stars. But it was also used by Andy Warhol to create what is probably to date the genre's only gay movie, *Lonesome Cowboys* (1968). Warhol made a neatly subversive use of what had become an instantly recognizable iconic location.

These are just some of the films, actors, writers, and directors I consider, but at all times, I want to create in *Straight* an eccentric text, one that refuses to adhere to the standard model of straight hegemonic discourse. I consider not only the films and the directors and the actors who made them, but the societal forces that shaped these performers and their works to give the reader some insight. I consider, for example, Jim Thompson's brutal childhood and adolescence; Kenneth Williams's fight for gay rights in Britain; and Robert Downey's quest to make films that intentionally outrage public sensibilities.

Toward the end of this volume, I touch briefly on the French film *Baise-moi* (*Rape Me,* 2000), directed by Coralie Trinh Thi and Virginie Despentes, from Despentes's popular novel of the same title. The film has created a predictable furor in the United States, but has been released throughout Western Europe (except in the United Kingdom and its home country, France) without much controversy. I was lucky enough to see the film for the first time during a visit to Amsterdam, where the film was shown at the Milkweg (a combination dance hall, live-theater workshop, and movie theater). It ran for an appreciative crowd of women and men who embraced the film's story of two young bisexual women on the run. Shunned by society, Manu (Raffaëla Anderson) and Nadine (Karen

Lancaume) go on a cross-country killing spree that is portrayed by the film as both exuberant and joyful in its random violence. Their target is the straight world and all who would question their love for each other, a love that is demonstrably real and faithfully foregrounded in the film, without any censorship compromises. The version playing in the United States did not escape customs without cuts; the version I saw was completely uncut, and was a riveting and liberating experience. No one in the audience during the screening of the film thought that it was in any way unusual; these were two women you didn't fuck with (literally).

In the United States, critics unfavorably compared the film to *Thelma & Louise* (1991), Ridley Scott's patronizing and patriarchal road movie in which Susan Sarandon and Geena Davis's characters drive off a cliff at the end of the film as a final act of rebellion, a rebellion that the film sees as foredoomed from the first frame. Though *Baise-moi* too ends in violent death, it is death on Manu and Nadine's terms, not terms imposed by a dragnet of state troopers pursuing them to their doom. If *Baise-moi* were about two men on the run, as *Butch Cassidy and the Sundance Kid* (1969) is, no one would question the ethos of the film, and it would be a huge hit. Two guys with guns are not threatening; they are just two grown-up kids playing games. Two women with automatics must be hunted down and destroyed. Straight society demands it.

Straight society sees those who reject its boundaries as violent, disruptive, sexually anarchic, selfish—not as players within the heterotopic regime. This is why lesbians and gay characters are routinely relegated to the roles of violent serial killers, drug dealers, hit men, sadistic siblings or parents, traitors—in other words, every form of human wreckage. This is the fear of the other. This is the reason for the Defense of Marriage Act. This is the reason for the continued enforcement of the straight lifestyle as the only choice that a responsible member of society can make. Yet straights may go to the movies and vicariously enjoy on-screen heterosexuality mixed with violence as one of the main staples of their cinematic diet, although pure performative sex is still relegated (no matter how consensual) to the realm of pornography.

CHAPTER ONE

※

Constructing Straightness

One may argue that, in contemporary cinema, visions of heterotopia no longer command the central portion of the narrative, which is now subsumed by unceasing violence and spectacle, the triumph of the disintegrated cyberbody over the reign of the idealized heterosexual couple. Recent television sitcoms, such as *Roseanne* and *Married . . . with Children,* have presented the family unit as a source of self-reflexive irony or a ghastly caricature. Today, when a "conventional" two-parent, two-children marriage is presented in contemporary cinema or television, it is almost always as a cynical joke; no one lives that way anymore. *Titanic* (1997) offers us Kate Winslet and Leonardo DiCaprio as the nominal love interests, but the real narrative is the spectacle of the foredoomed *Titanic* breaking up—the pornography of death. Martha Stewart marketed heterotopia as an empire (Martha Stewart Omnimedia) even as her own family unit imploded; Madonna has children but seems singularly detached from domesticity, despite her recent marriage to director Guy Ritchie; Rosie O'Donnell is a single mother who openly rejects the heterosexually based family model.

The era that produced *My Three Sons, I Love Lucy, Eight Is Enough, I Married Joan,* and *Bachelor Father* has been replaced with one that portrays stylish dysfunctionality in *Judging Amy, Sex and the City, The Sopranos,* and other teleseries that articulate what has become more than obvious: the heterosexually based model, though still desperately advertised in

Notting Hill (1999), *Miss Congeniality* (2000), *Say Anything* (1989), *While You Were Sleeping* (1995), and other mainstream films, is crumbling beneath the weight of its own imagistic prison. Indeed, one might well argue that the contemporary fascination with the serial killer has replaced audience interest in the conventional love story, with films like *Silence of the Lambs* (1991), *Se7en* (1995), *Kalifornia* (1993), and *Natural Born Killers* (1994) dominating the contemporary landscape. In this wilderness of pain, the heterosexual couple that *does* stay together is treated as a curiosity rather than as a commonplace. When, on *Sex and the City,* one of the protagonists gets married, the marriage turns out to be a sham: her partner is impotent. Families collapse in front of our eyes on *The Jerry Springer Show;* the "highlights" of the social implosions are then recycled on *Talk Soup.* JonBenét Ramsey's murder brings to the public's attention the spectacle of the overtly sexualized young girl, paraded through an endless grind of infant "beauty pageants" as a grim rehearsal for the performative arena of adult heterosexuality. It is now disaster rather than visions of heterosexual couplehood that compels audiences. The list is endless: Phil Hartman, murdered by his wife, Brynn, in 1998; John Belushi, dead of a drug overdose in 1982; the 380–pound, thirty-three-year-old Chris Farley, the Fatty Arbuckle of the 1990s, also dead of a drug overdose; Garrett Morris, shot by a gunman during a robbery in 1994; James Dean, Jayne Mansfield, Montgomery Clift, and Grace Kelly, all involved in fatal or near-fatal car crashes; Marvin Gaye, shot by his father; Kurt Cobain, dead by shotgun suicide on 7 April 1994; Latina pop star Selena, shot by a fan in 1995; Buddy Holly, Rick Nelson, and John Denver, all killed in plane crashes; television's Superman, George Reeves, dead from a mysterious gunshot wound in 1959; Natalie Wood, Freddie Prinze, Sr., Rebecca Schaeffer, David Strickland, John Candy, Sharon Tate, all dead through accident, violence, or misfortune; Rock Hudson, Amanda Blake, Raymond St. Jacques, Ray Sharkey, Tony Richardson, Robert Reed, Peter Allen, Liberace, and Tony Perkins, all victims of AIDS. The sad litany of tabloid fodder goes on and on, enthralling audiences who feel that, because misfortune befalls others, they will no longer be at risk. It is proof of their own existence, their continued survival. "Happily ever after" has become an ironic catch phrase, an unattainable state of grace.

Consider Tom Green and Drew Barrymore. Tom Green created a statue of his mother and father having sex and put it on the front lawn of his parents' home. Despite his father's anger, he subsequently spray-painted the hood of his parents' car with an image of two women making love. When Green was diagnosed with testicular cancer, it became the "hook" for an hour-long television special during which, perversely, we were allowed to see in clinical detail the surgery removing Green's cancerous testicle (we were denied, however, the opportunity to view a diagnostic procedure that detects testicular cancer in young men at an early stage of its progression). When Green and Drew Barrymore got married, they staged the ceremony as a publicity stunt on *Saturday Night Live;* Barrymore failed to appear. Subsequently, the couple were married in a private ceremony. We *think.* Green and Barrymore's courtship is thus a heterotopic parody of the notion of the traditional "married couple." In love, as in all other matters, they are *actors* first. Green relentlessly mines his own personal life, and the lives of those around him, for new material. He even wrote, produced, directed, and starred in *Freddie Got Fingered* (2001), a semiautobiographical feature film starring the always-game Rip Torn as his overbearing fictional father.

Nostalgia pervades not only *That '70s Show,* but also such films as *Saving Private Ryan* (1998), *U-571* (2000), and the teleseries *Band of Brothers*—anything to avoid the present. World War II, particularly, has become a safe haven for those who would seek to escape contemporary life; it has been transmogrified into a zone of heroes, martyrs, larger-than-life conflicts, and heterosexual romance. Vietnam remains contested ground, as such films as *Apocalypse Now* (1979, revised 2001), *Platoon* (1986), *Born on the Fourth of July* (1989), *The Walking Dead* (1995), and *The Green Berets* (1968) readily attest, but the dim presence of World War II can be reshaped at will to fit present-day marketing concerns. David Germain of the Associated Press reported on 22 May 2001, two days before the release of Michael Bay's *Pearl Harbor,* that

> The war spectacle "Pearl Harbor" will play in slightly revised form in Japan and Germany, where some dialogue is being tweaked to avoid offending audiences.
>
> Disney, which is releasing the film under its Touchstone Pictures banner, decided to alter some dialogue for the Japanese and German markets, said a Disney source, who spoke on condition of anonymity. . . .
>
> Though the film recounts Japan's sneak attack on Pearl Harbor in 1941, Disney hopes the movie will play well among Japanese audiences because of the love story at the heart of the film. (Germain)

Pearl Harbor, then, really is not about the attack on the Hawaiian naval base at all; it is the story of a romantic triangle that plays out with the attack as a backdrop. *Pearl Harbor* represents a nostalgic throwback to heterocentric World War II movies, but it is a hybrid. Here the romantic triangle competes with the spectacle of violence that audiences have come to expect. This hybrid spectacle-romance also differs from the films of the 1940s because it must play well in foreign markets. Desperate to please an older generation that still believes in heterocentrism and nationalism, a younger audience that is cynical of older values (even if they are nostalgic for them), not to mention myriad international audiences seeking an American product rife with violence and romance, *Pearl Harbor* hybridizes values of the past with the spectacle of the postmodern present. Disregard the realities of the situation if need be; one must, no matter what cuts are necessary, deliver the foreign market. As we redouble our colonial efforts on an actual scale in American foreign policy, we now repeat them on an imagistic scale in the zone of commerce. We can deliver whatever kind of World War II the customers require, particularly to our former enemies.

Furthermore, we will do it in such a way that our copyright on the material is faithfully perceived. Films were once released seasonally around the globe in distribution waves, gradually making their way through all potential markets. In the digital era, an age of instant piracy, films are now simultaneously or nearly simultaneously released in all territories to forestall the efforts of those who would seek illegally to appropriate Hollywood's vision. Beyond theatrical release, when films are recycled as DVDs after their initial run, they are produced as DVDs in rigid "coding" patterns to preserve the territorial integrity of the product being distributed. There are six DVD zones, or regions, as they are known: region one is the United States and Canada; region two is Western Europe and Japan; region three is Southeast Asia; region four is Latin America and Australia; region five is Russia, the rest of Asia, and Africa; and region six belongs solely to China. The racism of this coding system is immediately obvious: while American and Canadian audiences are assured immediate access to newly released films on DVD, a citizen of any country in Africa will have to wait up to a year to see a DVD coded for release in her or his country alone, because movies from region one (USA and Canada) will not play on a DVD player for regions two to six. Region one discs will play only on region one DVD players, region two discs will play only

on region two DVD players, and so on. Movies are released in DVD format at different times around the world, with America and Canada typically getting first access, then Australia and Japan six months later, Europe
twelve months after the initial release, and Africa eighteen months to two
years later. In some instances, movies are available for purchase in America and Canada as DVDs before they are released in European cinemas.
Due to the easily copied digital quality of DVDs and to the movie release
system used by Hollywood, these six regions were established to prevent
people from watching region one movies before they were released in
regions two to six, thus keeping a firm grip on the international video
rental and sales market. Certain filmmakers, in particular George Lucas,
have refused to release their films on DVD because the image and sound
quality is such that bootleg clones can be made at will. Indeed, one of the
attractions of digital technology is that every copy is as good as the original; thus, the term *original* becomes relatively meaningless. For this reason, Hollywood argues, the marketing of and access to DVDs has to be
strictly monitored, and if Third World countries are the last to be considered, one can say that this is just another echo effect of the heterocentrism and racism pervading Hollywood cinema as a whole. Just as the
makers of *Pearl Harbor* seem desperate to update and reaffirm crumbling
heterocentric master narratives, distributors, in the face of globalism,
seem desperate to control fragmenting yet expanding markets.

The trading of images and sounds over the Web has exploded in the
first years of the new century, followed by a flurry of lawsuits. Napster has
been effectively neutralized; Scour, a Los Angeles-based service that
allowed its users to trade "music and movies over the Internet" (Richtel
B4), was also forced to change its original access policies. One can, of
course, access theatrical trailers (heavily encrypted) over the Internet, but
the initial wave of free access available on the Web in the mid to late
1990s is now instead a series of strictly protected commercial access sites,
which provide consumers with less information each day at higher cost.
Advertisements, once rare on the Web, have become ubiquitous.

Even formerly ad-free print zones have been invaded by advertisers
eager to target every possible segment of the market. As James MacKinnon notes,

> In March, for the first time in almost 50 years, *Mad* magazine ran ads.
> Announcing the change with a cutesy disclaimer, the new owners at

> AOL-Time Warner jumped over the dead body of founder Bill Gaines and decided the crucial . . . demographic was too good to pass up. *Mad* always sold junk, but only *Mad* junk. Now it's selling its readers—to the people who make corn nuts, PlayStation, CDs and Cheez Whiz. (84)

Indeed, *Mad,* first as a comic book and later as a black-and-white newsstand magazine, was one of the few media voices in the 1950s openly to challenge McCarthyism, rampant consumerism, Hollywood excess, and the general vulgarity and shallowness of American culture. *Mad* also consistently critiqued the heterotopic ideal of marriage and the supposedly normative values of heterosexual conduct. Who will critique these concepts in the new century? The increasing multiconglomeratization of all aspects of print, television, cable, and film media makes it even more unlikely that dissenting voices will be tolerated, or even allowed to exist. In a marketplace where ideas and images are controlled almost solely by a few major companies, with hundreds of millions of dollars riding on every roll of the entertainment dice, criticism can no longer be permitted. Cross-plugging of films and books by television, radio, print ads, Web banner ads, direct mail, "spam" e-mail, and other avenues is now so routine as to create a new, artificial coherence out of the product being marketed. Movies are no longer individual entities; they are marketing events.

Just as films are marketed for a heterosexual audience, so too are the stars that appear in these films. Matthew Modine, Nicole Kidman, Ben Stiller, Drew Barrymore, and numerous other contemporary actors must conform to rigidly constructed body and facial "typings" to attain and maintain stardom. Wardrobes are carefully selected, hair is coifed to perfection, and publicity photographs are constructed under the most scrupulous supervision. Those who cross the meticulously crafted gender "drag" line do so at their peril. Tony Perkins was forever typecast as Norman Bates after his cross-dressing performance in *Psycho* (1960). Yet another, more phantasmal figure, represents a significant force in the rupture of sexual dress and performance stereotypes.

In 1961, inspired by the success of Alfred Hitchcock's film, William Castle (and his scenarist, Robb White) created the peculiar and disturbing film *Homicidal.* The plot of the film is predictably complex, but the central point of my argument here is that two of the leading characters, Emily (a woman) and Warren (a man) are both played by Jean Arless, a woman in real life. Throughout much of the film, Emily has center stage

FIGURE 1. *Left to right*: Patricia Breslin, Eugenie Leontovich, and Jean Arless as Emily in a dystopian family scene from William Castle's *Homicidal*. Courtesy: Jerry Ohlinger Archives.

as a rampaging, psychotic, bleached-blond murderer, who kills without compunction. Warren, on the other hand, is presented as a reasonable if somewhat unattractive young man, whom everyone in the film's narrative accepts as male. During the climax, Warren lures a young woman into a deserted house at night and then ritually disrobes, removing the men's clothing she has worn through most of the film and revealing herself as the scripted construct of Emily. Up until this point in the narrative, Castle and Robb have skillfully withheld the information about Arless's double role from both the audience and the characters in the film, so Arless's abandonment of her transgendered performative role comes as a shock to both the audience and the film's other protagonists. "Now do you know me?" Warren/Emily asks his intended victim, Miriam (Patricia Breslin), speaking in a man's voice while clothed in a white chiffon dress. As Miriam looks on in horror, Warren/Emily inserts a set of false front teeth in her mouth and removes her wig with deliberate accuracy. "Now . . . ?" he/she questions Miriam again. Unable to believe the spectacle she is witnessing, Miriam screams with horror as the male/female construct of Warren/Emily moves in for the kill and attempts to stab Miriam to death with a stiletto. Naturally, Miriam's fiancé, Karl (Glenn Corbett) saves her at the last minute, and Warren/Emily dies in the ensuing struggle. Yet what makes *Homicidal* so compelling today is its careful rehearsal and construction of performative body tropes adopted by Jean Arless in her portrayal of Warren; dressed in a business suit, with tie and suspenders, hands habitually thrust into trouser pockets, Warren is every bit the assured and aggressive masculine stereotype so ubiquitous in the heterocentric cinema of the 1900s to the present. As Emily, clad in a white gown—complete with gloves—flirting with Karl and warming milk in a saucepan for her paralyzed caregiver (a neat switch in itself), Arless projects the servitude and "femme" persona of a Donna Reed or a Jane Wyatt, the homemaker with murder in her heart.

Above all, *Homicidal* is about repression: Emily is forced to conceal her true identity in the character of Warren, who is seen as an icon of stability through much of the film. Warren asks Miriam at one point in the film, "What do we really know about anybody?"—implicitly acknowledging the duality of his/her identity and the intrinsic slippage of gendered performative norms. At the same time, Warren contains the murderous violence of Emily, let out of the prison of male drag to perform acts of violence, so that Warren can inherit a fortune from his dead father.

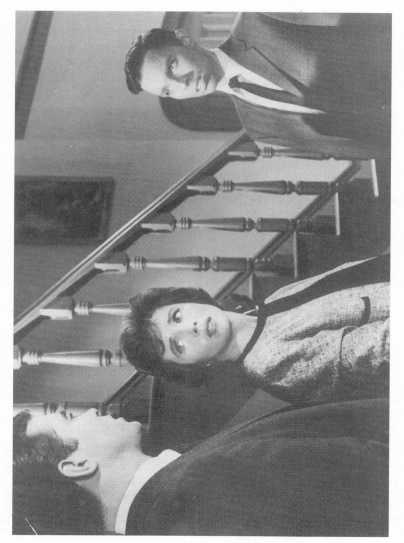

FIGURE 2. "What do we really know about anybody?": Glenn Corbett, Patricia Breslin, and Jean Arless as Warren in William Castle's *Homicidal*. Courtesy: Jerry Ohlinger Archives.

As we learn more about Warren/Emily's childhood, we discover that as Warren, the young "boy" was viciously beaten by his father to make him "more of a man," until the father died. Warren left for an extended stay in Sweden and then returned to claim the family fortune with the newly created Emily persona as his assistant. Castle manages to carry off this gender-bending deception seamlessly for eighty-two of the film's eighty-seven-minute running time, and indeed, just as Miriam is about to enter the house at the film's climax to be confronted by Warren/Emily, Castle, for the only time in the film, adopts a first-person point of view so that both the audience and Miriam enter the house together. To further call attention to the nature of the gender rupture about to be unveiled, Castle momentarily freezes the image just as we are about to enter the house and superimposes the image of a clock ticking off sixty seconds (accompanied by the sound of an amplified heartbeat), while warning the audience in a stentorian voice-over that this is their "last chance" to leave before the secret of Warren/Emily's double identity (which we do not yet know) is revealed. "Ten more seconds, and we're going into the house," Castle warns the viewer. As the seconds run out, Castle tells the viewers that they are "a brave audience" and picks up the tracking shot, taking us into the house to meet Warren in drag, or Emily in drag, with knife poised; but which is it? In the film's final shot, Castle splits the screen and presents the viewer with Warren on the left, immaculately dressed in male attire, and Emily on the right, the perfect vision of 1950s performative femininity. A superimposed title reads only "Introducing Jean Arless," so even though the film's narrative has properly concluded, the question of Arless's gender remains in flux.

In fact, Jean Arless is itself a pseudonym for Joan Marshall (1931–92), whose other films include *Shampoo* (1975), *The Horse in the Grey Flannel Suit* (1968), *Tammy and the Doctor* (1963), *Looking for Love* (1964), and *Live Fast, Die Young* (1958). Joan Marshall was also a frequent guest in numerous teleseries of the 1950s and 1960s, including *Star Trek, Petticoat Junction, The Munsters, The Twilight Zone, Hawaiian Eye,* and *Maverick.* Married for a time to director Hal Ashby, who directed *Shampoo,* Joan Marshall also wrote sitcoms, appeared on television variety shows, and worked as a showgirl at nightclubs in the 1950s in both Chicago and Las Vegas. After Ashby's death in 1988, Joan married business executive Mel Bartfield and eventually moved to Jamaica, where she spent her last days. Only thirty years old when she appeared in *Homici-*

dal, Joan Marshall/Jean Arless agreed to do the role only if her true identity, along with her sexual identity, remained a secret, and for someone
accustomed to accessorizing her body as a Las Vegas performer, her performative drag act in *Homicidal* was apparently fairly easy.

Tony Perkins, a bisexual man, was forced to reprise his role as Norman Bates in a series of increasingly dreary sequels (1983, 1986, 1990),
and he never really escaped the iconic straitjacket of the role. Jean Arless,
however, along with her roles as Warren and Emily, effectively vanished
with the last frames of *Homicidal.* Joan Marshall thus remains one of the
most curious and compelling examples of heterosexual performativity in
cinema. She created a new persona for herself as an actor solely for one
film, and then constructed two characters of different sexes within that
same film; all of them would disappear once filming had been completed.
As a symbol of performative sexual division within the hermetically sealed
world of late 1950s-early 1960s heterosexuality, Marshall's triple personality transformation is simultaneously disturbing and instructive: all is
drag, even one's personal identity.

Yet the construction of Jean Arless as a site of heterosexual dis-ease
pales in comparison to a new, entirely synthetic group of performers
who are created entirely out of pixels. Requiring hundreds of hours of
time plotting points on a computer screen, these are the virtual actors
of the future.

> Dr. Aki Ross, the young female protagonist of *Final Fantasy,* Columbia Pic-
> tures' new science-fiction epic, has the sinewy efficiency of Sigourney
> Weaver in *Alien* and the curves of Julia Roberts in *Erin Brockovich.* . . . That
> achievement is remarkable considering that Aki is no more than a computer
> animation. . . . Last month, Aki edged out dozens of real-life models and
> starlets to become the cover girl on Maxim's "Hot 100.". . . The same com-
> puter wizards who rendered her digitally in the estimated $100 million
> *Final Fantasy* stripped her down to a string bikini for Maxim.
>   Then there is Webbie Tookay, the latest lithesome discovery of John
> Casablancas, the founder of Elite Model Management, which shaped the
> careers of Cindy Crawford and Naomi Campbell. Webbie exists only in
> cyberspace, the creation of a Swedish animator named Steven Stahlberg, but
> that didn't hinder her from posing for a feature in Details in October, 1999,
> and a new Nokia phone advertising campaign in Latin America.
>   "Webbie can eat nothing and keep her curves," boasted Mr. Casablancas,
> who left Elite and founded Illusion 2K, an agency dedicated to representing

virtual models. "She can be on time, or in two places at one time, and you know she will never get a pimple or ask for a raise. Sometimes I wish all models were virtual.". . . "Think of Madonna or Michael Jackson," said Marsha Kinder, a professor of critical studies at the University of Southern California. "What's so distinctive about these stars is the malleability of their image. They are constantly reinventing themselves in a way that makes them seem like virtual figures. We even talk about them as though they were virtual, and why not? In our postmodern culture, a simulacrum is not only acceptable, it is preferable."

"People are fine with fake now," said Andrew Niccol, the writer, director and producer of *Simone,* a movie-in-progress, due out from New Line Cinema next fall[;] . . . the film's story line seems prescient: a virtual star replaces the leading lady (Winona Ryder) after she stalks off the set.

"Very soon we will be able to turn on our television sets and not know if the presenter is fake or real," Mr. Niccol said, "and frankly we won't care." (LaFerla B8)

Needless to say, these new synthetic performers will be absolutely "perfect" in their bodily proportions. They will be fantasy projections designed to appeal to men and women in a directly sexual manner. Not only is the heterosexual orientation of Webbie Tookay and Aki Ross a construct of their perceived social space, the synthespians themselves have been created to embody sites of heterosexual desire, without risk, imperfection, or involvement. It is the logical extension of the men's magazine pullout photo, once airbrushed to perfection; how unsightly bulges are eliminated through the use of Photoshop and other computer graphics programs. Why should one work from an imperfect original when sculpted, packaged, sterile "beauty" is so easily manufactured? With these new computer images of idealized heterotopia as a guide, more and more conventional performers, and viewers, will seek to trade in their human flaws for the body shaping offered by plastic surgery.

Already there is a public outcry over the artificial thinness of female performers, in particular, who must constantly maintain absurdly draconian diets to keep their weight to an absolute minimum. With a new, impossibly idealized standard to live up to, how can humans hope to compete? Even now, actual human models are being "cloned" in cybernetic doubles, so that their images can do double duty in multiple print and Internet ads. John Casablancas of Elite Model Management recently "cloned" the model Tatiana Rossi, christening her cyberdouble Adrenalina. He envisions the clone alternating with Ms. Rossi to endorse products on the Internet, in print and in public appearances, the last as a projection on a movie screen. "Through this type of manipulation we're going to completely confuse people," he said. . . . But the cyberbabe's extreme malleability has raised the ire of feminists. Virtual females are "the postmodern equivalent of a mail-order bride," scoffed Suzanna Walters, director of the feminist studies program at Georgetown University. "They are compliant creatures created for one's pleasure, another example of the female as object," and, worse, Ms. Walters suggested, an ideal that real women cannot hope to emulate. (LaFerla B8)

These plastic spokesphantoms, created to appeal to the heterosexual male consumer-viewer, remind one of the artificial perfection posited by Thorstein Veblen. Veblen commented that the effects generated by these heterosexually based images "are pleasing to us chiefly because we have been taught to find them pleasing[;] . . . if beauty or comfort [are] achieved . . . they must be achieved by means and methods that commend themselves to the great economic law of wasted effort" (51). These are the images the young boys and girls have been force-fed since childhood in an avalanche of artificial desire and objectificational constructs culled from television advertisements, print ads, magazine spreads, Internet sites, theatrical motion pictures, and other sources, cuing heterosexuals to respond to certain body types, hairstyles, and facial expressions that simultaneously suggest malleability and vacancy of spirit. We have been taught to find these fantasy females pleasing, and rather than challenge these stereotypes, Hollywood and its allies seek to perpetuate feminine (and masculine) objectification even at the cost of discarding the real. Indeed, one can argue that this has been their ambition all along; they only lacked the technology to do it. There is also no question that these phantom pitchwomen conform to Veblen's dictum that "they must be achieved by means and methods that commend themselves to the great economic law of wasted effort."

What could be more wasteful than the production of a commercial or a print ad? Ten hours to achieve one close-up of an eye. Body doubles hired for their hands, feet, or breasts. Food, clothing, cars, leisure activities all presented in images that take thousands of hours and miles of videotape and/or film to capture. If the average ratio of a conventional feature film is seven or eight to one (meaning seven or eight wasted minutes for each minute on the screen), commercials push this ratio into the range of one hundred to one, or even higher, because, no matter how much material and time is expended in the pursuit of these fleeting images, they must, if they are to be effective sales tools, be "perfect." As Hollywood budgets routinely balloon into the eighty- to one-hundred-million-dollar range for large-scale action features, we should remember that, in terms of money expended per second, commercials cost on the average twenty times as much as films to produce. The end result is ten seconds of film, or thirty seconds, but the terrific waste that goes into the creation of these snippets of images is justified by their sheer visual extravagance. To commodify leisure and desire, much less to conflate them into one marketable unit, requires a prodigious squandering of time, material, and human resources. Now, however, we can do it without the human element. We only need the computer technicians, who will labor in the dark, day after day, to bring these artificial arbiters of heterosexual desire into the contemporary imagistic marketplace. And their labor is cheap—interns will work for practically nothing, convinced that, by mastering the tools of simulacrum production, they will assure themselves a place in the new cybernetic economy, where on-screen talent is at last (the revenge of the producers) dispensable. Will we really recognize the difference? The technology is still relatively crude at the present moment, but six months from now? three years from now? Who can say that the synthespians will not replace the humans in the zone of entertainment and commerce that is the moving image in the dawn of the twenty-first century?

While pioneering Internet movie sites (such as Icebox, IFilm, Pop, Shockwave, Mediatrip, and Wirebreak), burned through millions of dollars in start-up capital and have been forced to reconfigure their business plans to survive in a media landscape that no longer finds the Web as alluring as an entertainment and/or advertising medium (Grover and Eads EB 126), the Web's place in the electronic marketplace is assured; it only needs fine-tuning. In addition to trailers, entire feature films, and digital cartoons circulating on the web, there has also been an explosion of live role-playing games that attract men and women alike. These offer the illusion of participation in a constructed hyperreality, available to one and all at a price. As AMC Entertainment, one of the nation's leading chains of movie theaters, cuts twenty percent of its 2,774 screens nationwide (that's 548 theaters being abandoned, to become skating rinks, grocery stores, warehouse outlets, or nightclubs) and Loews Cineplex chops

675 of its 2,967 screens because of decreased public demand for a night out at the movies ("AMC"), home video viewing (using TiVo, DVDs, and other nascent technologies), is on the rise. On-line and rental video games are becoming the entertainment medium of choice for many younger viewers. Yet, as Emily Laber found out, men and women want very different types of satisfaction from their gaming experience. Ultima Online, for example, has strong appeal for women gameplayers, and designers of video games are taking note of this new trend away from the standard "shoot 'em up" strategy of the more primitive games.

> "What women are finding so interesting about these games is that they provide a sense of community and social structure that you don't see in other games," [says] Patricia Pizer, a lead designer at Turbine Entertainment Software. . . .
>
> Officials at the companies that make the three most popular games [among women]—Ultima Online, from Origin Systems; Asheron's Call; and EverQuest, from Sony—said they did not design the games with women in mind and have been surprised at the response. (Laber D1)

Not that this would surprise Ernest Adams, a video-game theorist who recently created Dogme 2001 (after Dogme 95, the realist-cinema movement conceived by Lars von Trier, Thomas Vinterberg, and other maverick film directors who were seeking to get back to the basics of film production, eschewing spectacle and special effects). Adams's manifesto consciously forbids the use of numerous popular video-game structures and opens with the simple slogan "technology stifles creativity." In Adams's world, there are no "Good-and-Evil battles, first person shooters, technical jargon . . . knights, elves, dwarves or dragons," or other customary visual tropes typically embraced by the game world (Taylor 13). Men are still entranced by Doom, Quake, and Lara Croft: Tomb Raider, although more thoughtful players use their gaming experience to forge relationships that can potentially extend into the real world. But for all participants, it is the interactivity of the video-game experience rather than the potentially passive escape offered by the dominant cinema that attracts them. Director Atom Egoyan observes that, in the future,

> There's going to be a generation of film students that's going to look up Antonioni on a Web site and see a clip and read a description without physically sitting through a screening. We were probably the last generation with

the notion of a graven image, where filmmaking and film watching were a very physical thing. If we wanted to understand movies, we had to commit ourselves. We had to be physically in a theater for the two hours that that took. (Rakoff 39)

When film students at Yale recently tried to produce a student feature film, they discovered that the only way they could pique student interest was to make a digital video porn film, so exhausted have conventional narrative structures and genre requirements become. The project grew out of an ad hoc student group of women and men that called itself Porn 'n Chicken; the members met regularly to "eat fried chicken and watch X-rated films" (Herszenhorn A21). Loosely based on the activities of a secret campus society, much like the real-life Skull and Bones, the proposed film generated a great deal of discussion on campus, although the actual production of the film occurred sporadically. Yet the producers of the film stated in their production manifesto that their desire in creating the film, tentatively titled *The StaXXX,* was to endow contemporary pornography with humanity and compassion, qualities notably absent from most commercial fare. Wrote the producers,

> Throughout viewing of the pornographic canon . . . we found that most depictions lacked the complexity and aesthetic beauty of the sexual experience as well as the intellectual aspects of seduction. . . . The "action sequences" [will] be conceptualized and scripted in collaboration with the actors themselves, to liberate the film from any sort of preconceived sexual agenda . . . [and] safe sex [will] be the exceptionless rule. . . . At this point, the movie will include heterosexual and homosexual sequences, as well as scenes exploring fetishism, group sex and non-physical intercourse. . . . A female junior who starred in the film's first scene called the producers serious and respectful. "I figured it was a 50–50 chance that it was a joke," she said, recalling her initial reaction. "I was pretty impressed with their organization and their professionalism, considering what they were trying to do is create a full-length adult film on a college campus with college kids."
>
> The woman, who is active in feminist issues on campus, was filmed having sex with a girlfriend. "They were not interested in getting the most hard-core stuff they could find," she said. "They were interested in college students doing what college students do. They were not going to tell us what they wanted. They were not going to direct that. It was the actors who got to choose." (Herszenhorn A21)

Thus, in this instance, students are taking back their own sexuality, which has long been the property of marketplace commodifiers, and are creating a group work that depicts their actual sexual orientation, devoid of the standard coupling ritual presented in commercially produced video porn. In moving beyond performative heterosexuality and beyond the artificially created normative values that have been inculcated in audiences for the past one hundred years, the students have used a new, lightweight, inexpensive technology to present their true selves to the world, without patriarchal scripting, without submitting to the power of the male or female gaze. Rather than being designed for the viewer, these films are designed for the participants, in the tradition of most experimental cinema, in which the creators, rather than audience demand, shape the vision of the work in question.

Projects like this Yale film serve as a radical and transgressive counteroffensive to most contemporary television programming, particularly on cable, which seems determined to satiate the (mostly male) viewer with a series of determinedly salacious, sex-themed programs. Home Box Office (HBO) offers *G-String Divas,* documenting the lives of a group of exotic dancers in a "gentlemen's club"; *Taxicab Confessions,* also on HBO, regales the viewer with oral narratives of sexual encounters and assignations with mind-numbing regularity. As critic A. J. Jacobs comments,

> [A]s networks compete with cable, and cable competes with the Internet, and everyone competes with R-rated antics on the big screen, it seems TV has sex on the brain. It's everywhere. Flip to *Ally McBeal* and see the under-the-knee orgasm trick. Check out *Friends,* where Chandler and Monica have all-day nooky sessions. Drink in Howard Stern's CBS show, where he slathers mayonnaise and bologna on a woman's naked tush. Look at MTV's new series *Undressed,* where, in the first episode, a character snuggles up to a seven-inch vibrator: And sample The WB's *Dawson's Creek, Buffy the Vampire Slayer,* and *Felicity,* where there's more deflowering going on than in a badly managed greenhouse. (22–23)

What is happening here is that, at long last, the mainstream television market has closed ranks with those who madeexploitation films from the 1910s through the 1970s. Unable to garner a significant audience share by any other means, network and cable executives have embraced sexuality as yet another marketable commodity. Such theatrical exploitation films of the classical theatrical era as *The Big Snatch* (1968),

The Head Mistress (1968), *The Notorious Daughter of Fanny Hill* (1966), *Trader Hornee* (1970), *Primitive Love* (1964), *Striporama* (1954), *Teaserama* (1955), *Varietease* (1954), and *Buxom Beautease* (1956), once relegated to the Forty-second Street grind-house circuit, are now readily available on television, either by channel subscription to HBO, Cinemax, and other pay services or on an individual film-on-demand basis on such cable networks as Spice. On the Playboy channel, a new hit show called *Night Calls 411* is indicative of the new highly sexualized cable programming being offered; as one might expect, the productions are both heterosexist and boringly predictable, as critic Frank Rich observed when invited to view a taping of the program. For both the performers and the viewers of *Night Calls 411,* performative heterosexuality is a readily transparent construct in which the "hosts" of the show interact with the members of their viewing audience as if acting out a fantasy of sexual contact rather than engaging in a personal encounter. As for the "adult" films available on DVD and videocassette from such major producers as VCA Pictures, Wicked Pictures, and other companies, they present a tawdry and ultimately machinelike vision of the body as the site of repetitive performance without passion, reflecting the absence of the body within the frame, or the triumph of the ritual of performative sex over human contact, plot, setting, genre, or stylistic affectation. As Rich notes, "[n]o matter what the period or setting, no matter what the genre, every video comes to the same dead halt as the performers drop whatever characters they're supposed to be assuming and repeat the same sex acts, in almost exactly the same way, at the same intervals, in every film" (82).

The commodification of sexual desire represented by the commercial (and highly profitable) porn industry is yet another symptom of the collapse of the empire of images created by the dominant Hollywood cinema in the twentieth century. The stars, the plots, the genres fail to satisfy. Each new film is merely an installment in a larger project that will take years, perhaps decades to complete (as in the *Star Wars, Star Trek,* and James Bond film series), with each new episode designed only momentarily to slake audiences' thirst for a believable, alternative universe, while simultaneously leaving them somehow dissatisfied, hoping for greater spectacle, exasperated with hypernarratives stuffed with action but devoid of humanity or any external human agency. How can we break free of this imagistic prison? Do we wish to? Or have we—both producers and audiences—forgotten how to dream with our eyes open? How did we get to this point in the first years of the new century?

As Jonathan Ned Katz has usefully pointed out, *heterosexuality* itself is a construct of fairly recent origin. In his book *The Invention of Heterosexuality*, Katz notes,

> The earliest-known use of the word *heterosexual* in the United States occurs in an article by Dr. James G. Kiernan, published in a Chicago medical journal in May 1892. . . . Dr. Kiernan's article also included the earliest-known U.S. publication of the word *homosexual*. The "pure homosexuals" he cited were persons whose "general mental state is that of the opposite sex." These homosexuals were defined explicitly as gender benders, rebels from proper masculinity and femininity. In contrast, his heterosexuals deviated explicitly from gender, erotic, and procreative norms. In their American debut, the abnormality of heterosexuals appeared to be thrice that of homosexuals. Though Kiernan's article employed the new terms *heterosexual* and *homosexual*, their meaning was ruled by an old, absolute reproductive ideal. His heterosexual described a mixed person and compound urge—at once sex-differentiated, eros-oriented, and reproductive. (Katz 19–20)

Once identified, this new oppositional binary found its most expressive model sheet in the nascent forms of early cinema. Alice Guy Blaché in 1896 created what many consider to be the first film with a narrative, *La Feé aux choux [The Cabbage Fairy]*. This charming one-minute film celebrates the birth of a child delivered by the Cabbage Fairy, the French mythological version of the American stork. One could not imagine a more thoroughly heterosexual scenario than this one, and it is significant that throughout much of Blaché's work, both marriage and childbearing are almost ceremonially invoked as symbols of status and sexual role differentiation. Other early pioneers, including Augustin Le Prince, were also creating early filmstrips that captured the performative heterosexualized human body in motion.

Working at approximately the same period, Georges Méliès, William Friese-Greene, Jean Aimé Le Roy, Grey and Otway Latham, Max and Emil Skladanowsky, and other film pioneers all made significant contributions to the emerging medium. It was Louis-Jean Lumière and his brother, Auguste-Marie-Louis-Nicolas Lumière, however, who made the final breakthrough in combining the photographic and projection device into one machine in early 1895. It was patented on 13 February 1895

(Ceram 142–49), and the first Lumière projections took place shortly thereafter. "On December 28, 1895, . . . the first public performance took place—in the Salon Indien of the Grand Café, Boulevard des Capucines 14 in Paris. . . . The admission was a franc. The first day brought in thirty-five francs; within a short time the takings increased to 300 francs per day" (Ceram 149–50).

The commercial future of the Lumières' device was assured. Birt Acres, an Englishman, patented his own motion picture camera and projection device, dubbed the Kineopticon, in May 1895. Like the Lumières, Acres was quick to exploit the moneymaking aspects of his device. He presented a series of short films to the public starting on 14 January 1896. Some of Acres's titles, such as *Sea Waves at Dover,* are reminiscent of the pastoral scenes recorded in the Lumière actualities, but other brief subjects, including *The Arrest of a Pickpocket,* seem to anticipate the exploitational vigor of Thomas A. Edison's later films. Max and Emil Skladanowsky also specialized in street scenes and brief "documentaries" of life in their native Berlin, but they failed to duplicate the Lumières' commercial success. The first real genius of commercial exploitation, of course, was Thomas Edison, who introduced heterosexual, or sexualized, spectacle into one of his first filmstrips. *Annabelle the Dancer* featured Annabelle Whitford Moore performing an energetic dance in a long flowing gown; the film was hand tinted in various colors for public exhibition. *Annabelle the Dancer* was shown at Koster and Bial's Music Hall in New York City on 23 April 1896, the first public projection of Edison's kinetoscopic films using Thomas Armat's device, the Vitascope. Edison had intended his films to be peep-show entertainments but soon changed his mind as he saw the commercial potential of projected motion pictures.

Indeed, one can argue that of all the early film pioneers, it was Edison and his associates who most clearly saw the profit potential of the new medium. Even early Edison films, like *Blacksmithing Scene* (1893) and *Horse Shoeing* (1893) were consciously staged events, not actualities of real events taken in the field. Edison's troupe of actors and technicians thus set about recreating the staged verisimilitude of existence, using a variety of spatial and visual tropes to achieve their goal. In such films as *The Barber Shop* (1893) and *Sandow* (1894), Edison designed hermetically sealed spaces to contain the human body and to draw the viewer's attention to it as a fetishized object. The most notable examples of this tendency to eroticize the human corpus within a rigidly stylized setting

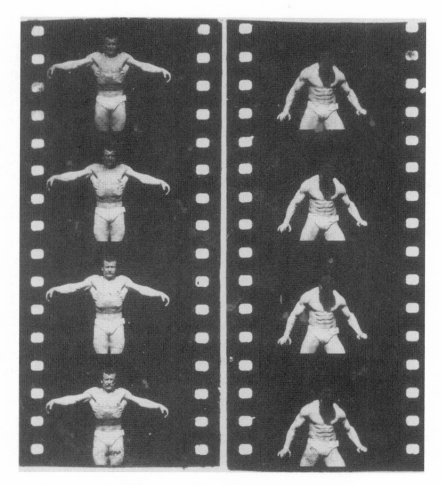

FIGURE 3. Eugene Sandow flexes his muscles for the gaze of Edison's camera in *Sandow.* Courtesy: Jerry Ohlinger Archives.

are Edison's films of the body in the act of performative play, such as the aforementioned *Sandow,* featuring muscleman Eugene Sandow flexing his muscles for the gaze of Edison's camera; and *Carmencita* (1894), a brief documentary of a Spanish dancer performing her highly charged routine for the delectation of a presumably male audience. Carmencita's dance routine "communicated an intense sexuality across the footlights that led male reporters to write long, exuberant columns about her performance" (Musser 34).

In the earliest films, there is no attempt to disguise the artificiality of the spectacle being created for and recorded by the camera. In this, Edison's first films are echoed by the early films of Andy Warhol, particularly *Couch* (1964), *Harlot* (1964), *The Life of Juanita Castro* (1965), and *Vinyl* (1965), in which props are stripped down to a minimalistic nothingness, and the black murkiness of the frame's backspace intentionally signifies the staged theatricality of the work. In all of Edison's films, it is the body—at work, at play, or preening for the camera—that is the center of our attention, in direct contrast to the work of the Lumières. As Musser comments,

> The Lumières' early films differ from Edison's in their approach to the body. Lumière films focus much more on landscapes and cityscapes. When people are subjects, they are seen in relationship to their background—situated in their world rather than extracted from it. More than bodies, Lumière films commodify landscapes and foreign locales within an imperialist culture. People are heavily clothed and usually stout— these are the bourgeoisie whose bodies are not subject to the discipline of factory labor. (43)

As late as 1898, Edison's technicians were still using minimal backgrounds or simply a black background to film *Serpentine Dance* (1897) and *Sun Dance* (1897), both starring the dancer Annabelle, as well as *Ella Lola, a la Trilby* (1898) and *Turkish Dance, Ella Lola* (1898). In such minimalistic settings, the performative heterosexualized body became the sole focal point of the viewer's attention. This last film became a celebrated censorship case when Ella Lola's suggestive body display was censored, in some versions, by the insertion of an optically superimposed grid, which covered the offending portions of her anatomy. In all of these films, Edison is consciously exploiting the nascent medium for as much novelty and notoriety as possible, in addition to establishing the "male gaze" that still dominates cinema practice more than a century later. Judith Mayne perceptively deconstructs the strategy at work in these early Edison films in her essay "Uncovering the Female Body."

> How convenient, and appropriate, that in one of the earliest Edison films, *Annabelle Butterfly Dance* (1895), a woman's clothing plays a central role. Dancing for the camera, the woman is dressed in billowing fabric that swirls about her, almost engulfing her at times. That the woman is performing for the camera is clear, but the movements of her body and the swirling fabric do not seem to be anchored in a specific context[;] . . . there is little distinction between the movements of the body and of the fabric. Put another way, the film, like the fabric, hides the female body while also displaying it. The simultaneous display and concealment could be read as a condition of the voyeuristic appeal of the cinema. (64)

The foregrounding of the performative human body in Edison's films in fact began with the inventor's first attempts at creating motion pictures, in a series of cylinder-drum experiments entitled *Monkeyshines No. 1, Monkeyshines No. 2,* and *Monkeyshines No. 3* (all 1890), created by Edison's two key associates, W. K. L. Dickson and William Heise (Musser 71–72). Other early films, including *Newark Athlete* (1891), *Men Boxing* (1891), *Man on Parallel Bars* (1892), *Fencers* (1892), *Wrestling* (1892), *Athlete with Wand* (1894), and *Unsuccessful Somersault* (1894), continued the Edison film factory's fascination with the body in motion, spatially and temporally separated from the world it ostensibly inhabits (Musser 71–89). But most interesting and compelling in Edison's early film work is the inventor's fascination with the display of this aestheticized body *at the expense of other entertainments* (which were introduced slightly later in Edison's career) and still centered on the male and/or female body as the site of the viewer's gaze.

As the novelty of captured motion wore off, Edison was pushed by economic need to create more bizarre entertainments, notably *Boxing Cats* (1894), in which two cats duke it out in a miniature boxing ring in a parody of the Edison "fight" films *Leonard-Cushing Fight* (1894) and *Boxing Match* (1894). Even in films that were devoid of violence, like *Highland Dance* (1894), Edison was constructing a gallery of body-display tropes that involved exaggerated masculinity (the boxing films), hyperstylized sensuality (the Ella Lola and Carmencita films), and the idealization of the heterosexual pairing of man and woman as a discrete

FIGURE 4. The heterosexualized female body of Carmencita in an early Edison filmstrip. Courtesy: Jerry Ohlinger Archives.

social unit. In subsequent films, Edison continued to pursue his interest in the bizarre and unusual as well, for he knew that, by appealing to the basest appetites of his viewers, he was simultaneously pursuing the surest avenue to commercial success. As Musser notes, Edison's films were "commercially corrupt from [the] beginning" (31), thus aligning the motion picture pioneer with later makers of exploitation films such as Russ Meyer, Roger Corman, and Doris Wishman, who sought to give the public what it wanted, even if that public was afraid—or too constrained by social boundaries—to articulate that desire. Thus Edison produced *Rat Killing* (1894), in which a dog leaps upon a group of large rats (specially purchased for the occasion at a cost of $32.30) and savagely kills them (Musser 123). This film was followed by no fewer than three sequels, *Rats and Terrier No. 2, Rats and Terrier No. 3,* and *Rats and Weasel;* all four films were shot on the same day in 1894 (Musser 123–24). In this, Edison was foreshadowing the now prevalent practice of shooting several sequels to a successful film simultaneously once a proven market has been established. Ever the master exploitationist, Edison knew what the public would pay to view, even adding the grotesque "novelty" of a weasel to replace the terrier in the last of the series, although in this case, the weasel was bested by the rats and the fourth film was never released (Musser 124).

Edison's racist and colonialist prejudices were also on transparent display, in such films as *Buffalo Bill* (a record of rifle shooting by the famed western "fighter"); *Sioux Ghost Dance* ("one of the most peculiar customs of the Sioux tribe is here shown," Edison's advertising copy exclaimed [Musser 125–26]); *Indian War Council* (in which Buffalo Bill "negotiates" with the Native Americans to maintain the peace); and *Buffalo Dance*. All of these were shot on the same day in the fall of 1894 (Musser 125–26). The exoticization and othering inherent in these manufactured narratives continued in such films as *Pedro Esquirel and Dionecio Gonzales [Mexican Knife Duel], Vincente One Passo [Lasso Thrower],* and *Sheik Hadji Taviar,* all shot on 6 October 1894 at Edison's Black Maria. Indeed, as can be seen from this hectic production pace, Edison was already anticipating the studio system of supply and demand, churning out new and highly commercial product on an assembly-line basis. Edison had set down the basic precepts upon which moving-image production, distribution, and exhibition are still based: give the audience spectacle, sex, and violence while simultaneously paying lip service to the dominant social order. Edison's early films

FIGURE 5. Thomas Edison's Black Maria, one of the world's first film-production facilities. Courtesy: Jerry Ohlinger Archives.

encoded a heterocentric world of idealized romantic couples, racist stereotypes, relentless exoticization, and othering of European, Asian, and
African culture, leavened with a healthy dose of sadism and voyeurism to
titillate the public.

While Edison was inventing, along with Étienne-Jules Marey,
Augustin Le Prince, the Lumières, and others, the foundation of the modern heterocentric motion picture, other early practitioners of the cinematic art were also creating worlds of their own invention. Georges
Méliès presented his trademark brand of phantasmagorical wizardry in
such films as *Le Spectre* (1899), *Le Rêve de Noël* (1900), *Le Voyage dans la
lune* (1902), and literally hundreds of other films in his Paris studio.
However, Méliès's

> earliest work was essentially a copy of [the Lumière brothers'] actuality films,
> but he then went on to make hundreds of westerns, fantasies, reenactments
> of news stories (most notably, the Dreyfus affair) and historical events (Joan
> of Arc's trial), children's pictures and "stag" films (i.e.[,] soft porn). In 1917,
> however, the army seized around 400 of these, and melted them down to
> make boot heels. Several years later, a cache of Melies [sic] films were dis-
> covered, most of which happened to be fantastical. These were shown at a
> retrospective, and henceforth, the name Melies has been synonymous with
> spectacle and primitivism. (Perry)

While Keith Perry is indeed correct that Méliès's output has been somewhat misrepresented, there is little doubt that some of his most compelling films are often disturbing heterosexual fantasies. In *Escamotage
d'une dame chez Robert-Houdin* (1896), Méliès makes a woman vanish
before our eyes; in *L'Hallucination de l'alchemiste* (1897), Méliès presents
the viewer with a gigantic star sporting five female heads; *Hallucinations
du Baron Munchausen* (1911) features a woman/spider construct reminiscent of the Scorpion King in *The Mummy Returns* (2001); and in *Le
Chaudron infernal* (1903), three young women are boiled alive in a gigantic cauldron. Méliès used women primarily as suggestive props in his
many films, and his films (often bootlegged) were popular with audiences
in both France and America ("Georges Méliès").

During this time, Winsor McCay had enormous success with his
one-reel animated cartoon *Gertie, the Trained Dinosaur* (1909): D. W.
Griffith and his cameraman Billy Bitzer were beginning their illustrious
careers with the Biograph Studio, starting with *The Adventures of Dollie*

(1908), Griffith's first film as a director. While foreign competitors were also making significant advances in film grammar and technology, Griffith and Bitzer created a dazzling series of one-reel and then gradually longer films, refining parallel editing, and the use of close-ups, fades, and dissolves. Films like *The Lonedale Operator* (1911), a classic example of intercutting for suspense, and *Fighting Blood* (1911) established Griffith's early reputation. His vision of American life, however, was hopelessly arcane, and his works are riddled with racism, sexism, and racial and cultural stereotyping.

Griffith's southern Victorianism largely escaped public notice until he produced and directed *The Birth of a Nation* (1915), a lavish spectacle of the Civil War in which the Ku Klux Klan were portrayed as heroes, and African Americans as fools, plunderers, and rapists. The storm of controversy surrounding the film has, quite justly, never dissipated, for despite its technical brilliance, *The Birth of a Nation* reminds the contemporary viewer of nothing so much as Leni Riefenstahl's Nazi-inspired *Triumph des Willens* (1934) and *Olympia* (1938). Griffith's attempts to defend himself in the equally lavish *Intolerance* (1916) proved commercially and critically disastrous, and the director finished out his career with melodramas, light comedies, and historical reenactments. Of his later work, only *Isn't Life Wonderful* (1924) and *Broken Blossoms* (1919) approach the inventiveness and intensity of his admittedly compromised work. But Griffith had served his chief function in cinema history: he had furthered the construction of the social fabric that Edison had first excavated and exploited. In Griffith's and Edison's films, there is no room in the dominant plot structure for women and/or minorities, except as victims and buffoons and occasionally villains. Griffith's vision of America's cultural melting pot, like that of Edison and his colleagues, was rigid and narrowly defined; it swept all nonheterosexual social discourse into the oblivion of marginalization. It is not too much to say that in these early films, both men created a blueprint for the dominant cinema that would be used up to the present day, with only minor challenges to its glyphic authority—and all of the challenges have been quickly incorporated into the system or relegated to the margins of cinematic discourse.

Fortunately, however, at the same time that Griffith was solidifying the code that continues to govern the representational and sexual rules of imagery in the cinema, a small but dedicated group of women was taking a different view of American life. The radical series of films they created demonstrate how differently the medium might have developed were it not for the patriarchal sexism and racism ingrained in the social fabric of the United States. Alice Guy Blaché left Gaumont studio after her early work in France to journey to America, where she created her own studio, Solax, located at Fort Lee, New Jersey. In an era dominated by D. W. Griffith, Thomas Edison, and Edwin S. Porter, Alice Guy Blaché (who had been directing at Gaumont from 1896 to 1905 as the company's sole auteur) turned her practiced hand to an ambitious series of films that directly confronted the social and cultural prejudices of her time. Solax was a functioning production entity from 7 September 1910 until June 1914, and during that time, it produced roughly two films per week, most of which Blaché directed. Among her many films for Solax were *The Violin Maker of Nuremberg* (1911), *Greater Love Hath No Man* (1911), *The Detective's Dog* (1912), *Canned Harmony* (1911), *A House Divided* (1913), and *Matrimony's Speed Limit* (1913; Slide 22). In *A House Divided,* a stereotypical heterosexual couple quarrel over a misunderstanding and refuse to speak to each other; they communicate only through written messages. In the end it is the woman (as in many of Blaché's films) who facilitates the couple's reconciliation. In *The Detective's Dog,* a rather ineffectual sleuth finds himself bound and gagged, tied to a log in a sawmill, and facing certain death, when his dog and fiancée break in and save him at the last minute—a neat reversal of the traditional maiden-in-distress formula so often used by Griffith.

Lois Weber was another women filmmakers in the early years of cinema. Her feminist tracts still surprise those viewers lucky enough to see them, offering as they do a refreshing alternative to the patriarchal dominant cinema of the period. Often working with her husband, Phillips Smalley, Weber created a canon of works that are both philosophical tracts and structurally sophisticated narratives. As Anthony Slide notes of this gifted filmmaker,

> Her films took stands on a wide variety of controversial matters: *Where Are My Children?* [1916] opposed abortion and advocated birth control. *The People vs. John Doe* [1916] was an indictment against capital punishment. *Hypocrites* [1915] attacked hypocrisy in our daily lives, in the church, politics, and in business. (34)

Many women in the silent era found a haven at Universal Pictures; they included Ruth Stonehouse, Ruth Ann Baldwin, and Ida May Park, who created a body of work that celebrates women's accomplishments in the private and public social spheres. Dorothy Davenport Reid directed and/or starred in several feature films in the early 1920s, after her husband, actor Wallace Reid, died on 18 January 1923 (he died at the age of thirty-one from morphine, to which he had become addicted following an automobile accident). Dorothy Davenport Reid used a male director in her films, but her guiding hand was very much in evidence on *Human Wreckage* (1923), loosely based on her husband's tragic life; *Broken Laws* (1924), "an attack on neglectful parents, who indulged their children" (Slide 76); and her best film, *The Red Kimono* (1926), the story of a young woman who marries a faithless man.

Frances Marion, whose main claim to fame is as a screenwriter with more than 150 screenplays and/or original stories to her credit, directed her first film, *Just Around the Corner,* in 1920. The film was favorably received, and Marion went on to direct and script *The Love Light* (1921), starring Mary Pickford. This film proved an enormous success, no doubt in part because of the presold value of Mary Pickford's iconic screen image, but Marion directed only one other film, *The Song of Love* (1923), which achieved only modest success. Following the production of *The Song of Love,* Marion turned her full attention to screenwriting, perhaps realizing that it was easier and more satisfying to write screenplays than to manage the cast and crew of a feature film. Dorothy Arzner made three silent films before beginning her long career in sound films: *Fashions for Women, Ten Modern Commandments,* and *Get Your Man* (all 1927).

The work of women filmmakers during the silent era conclusively demonstrates that, during the formative years of the medium, there was indeed an alternative to that vision of the contemporary dominant cinema then being practiced in Hollywood. Also, especially in the cases of Alice Guy Blaché and Lois Weber, this feminist vision offered viewers something they would never have the opportunity to experience again: a visual dialogue between men and women on matters of race, gender, equality, and social standing. (There are, however, unfortunate racist moments in Blaché's work. In *Matrimony's Speed Limit,* African American stereotypes are used for predictably racist "humor," much to the viewer's dismay. In addition, a Blaché film discovered by David Navone in 2000, *A Fool and His Money* [Solax, 1912], is a decidedly racist comedy—despite revisionist claims to the contrary [Silents Majority]—featuring an entirely segregated African American cast, including "Cakewalk King"

James Russell. These defects of vision are regrettable and mar the otherwise egalitarian spirit of Blaché's work as a whole.)

Nevertheless, the creative and performative freedom that women filmmakers enjoyed during the silent era was a result of the relative youth of the medium. No one really expected, when Blaché began directing in 1896, that the cinema would eventually develop into a multibillion-dollar-a-year business, controlled by banks and corporate interests and designed almost exclusively to appeal to the least-discriminating viewer. The silent era was a period of fermentation and experimentation; for a time, it seemed that anything was possible as long as it made money at the box office. But even as early as 1908, when Florence Lawrence moved from Biograph to Carl Laemmle's Independent Motion-Picture Company and set into motion the star system as we know it today, new boundary lines were being drawn.

As men seized control of a now-profitable business, women found themselves excluded from the decision-making process, in addition to being commodified as objects of desire for mass consumption. And physical typecasting became commonplace. John Bunny, for example, was the initial prototype of the rotund comedian who gets laughs because of his girth and his willingness to allow audiences to laugh at his obesity. After John Bunny, such stars as Fatty Arbuckle, Lou Costello, John Belushi, Chris Farley, and John Candy carried on this tradition, usually with disastrous results to their health. Sexually ambiguous, these comedians' physical bulk placed them in a peculiar situation within the iconic structure of the Hollywood cinema. Ostensibly "straight," all of these men were essentially asexual, and their physical desires were often (if not always) used as the creative source material for cruel and demeaning jokes at their own expense. Maurice Costello, on the other hand, was one of the first movie idols; his refined and cultured screen personality made him the adored sexual object of millions of women (and certainly some men). Charles Ray was typed ruthlessly as a green country boy in a series of rural comedies; decades later the naïve and bumptious Joe E. Brown filled the role. Francis X. Bushman, whose career spanned six decades (his final role was a bit part in *The Ghost in the Invisible Bikini* [1966]), formed the cinema's first great love team with his then-wife, Beverly Bayne. Perhaps the most notorious case of typecasting was that of Mary Pickford, whose image as an on-screen juvenile was so indelibly etched in the public's collective mind that, long after she had grown to adulthood, she was still forced to play the ingénue on specially constructed sets, using oversized props. Charles Chaplin's tramp character became an overnight sensation, catapulting the ex-vaudevillian into the stratosphere of Hollywood society and the freedom of his own studio. There he could pursue his projects in splendid isolation and even ignore, for a time, the advent of sound. Douglas Fairbanks, Sr., was one of the screen's first heterosexualized swashbucklers; in later years, Errol Flynn and others would imitate his hypermasculinized vigor and dashing charm, all in the service of a screen image that clearly marked him as an active heterosexual.

As films became more formulaic in response to the law of supply and audience demand, they had to be made more and more quickly, and character typing became the rule rather than the exception. Where once Lois Weber could experiment on a film like *Hypocrites* with the resources of a major studio behind her, no one seemed willing to take chances anymore. The dominant white heterocentric cinema became the genre cinema, with a predictable series of characters and situations leading to a preordained climax, with only slight variation. Films were made and remade as studios strove to cut production costs to the bone by utilizing the same source material two, three, even five times or more. Westerns used the same plot over and over again: the lone gunman rides into town, finds the situation intolerable, and cleans up the den of thieves before moving off into the sunset, with or without a love interest. Motivation and characterization were seen as irrelevant; what audiences wanted was familiarity, both in the stars they worshipped and in the construction of the heterocentric narratives in which the stars appeared. Make no mistake about it: audiences created these stars and genres by voting with their feet and their pocketbooks. When they liked a personality (however manufactured) or a genre (be it westerns, "exotic" films, slapstick comedies, or rural dramas), producers took note and supplied them with more of the same. This pattern would continue until the genre had been exhausted, at which point it would usually fall into burlesque. Then, at last, the format would be laid to rest for a while, until a new approach would arise to resuscitate the formula, and the entire cycle of rise and decay would be repeated anew.

Feminine figures of desire had to be pure, heterosexual, and white. Names were bland and interchangeable, just as the characters and the plots of the films themselves were interchangeable: Olga Cronk had to be reborn as Claire Windsor, and Lucille Vasconcellos Langhanke would go on to fame and fortune as Mary Astor. Thus Mary Pickford, Louise

Lovely, Arline Pretty, and other silent screen heroines projected an image of sweetness and light, untouched by the taint of sexual desire; they were unattainable icons of the male heterosexual quest. Early leading men were equally straitjacketed, being invariably white, in their mid-to-late twenties, possessed of resolve and stern moral fiber. They embodied all the puritan values of the late-nineteenth century in one neat, also unattainable, icon of heterosexual desire. For both men and women, their idealized screen "selves" represented archetypes of impossible virtue, a façade that could only be perpetuated by continual repression and denial. Carlyle Blackwell, Dustin Farnum, King Baggott, and Harold Lockwood were all early exemplars of this utterly unrealistic masculine image.

Apparently, the offspring of these idealized heterosexual couples often came to grief, for it was the constructed *desire* of heterosexuality, not its issue, that was commodified in early cinema. If children were introduced into the narrative structure, they were either wide-eyed innocents or, if in their adolescence or early childhood, cheerful rapscallions. Teenagers, then as now, inevitably meant trouble and rebellion against the moral high ground their parents had so assiduously sought. Fathers were increasingly marginalized from this phantasmal world; it seemed as if the idealized couples of the romance film went straight from courtship to a series of spectacularly dysfunctional unions, in which men were either absent or portrayed as unreasoning tyrants. Villains, then as today, were marked by a complete lack of virtue—the dark, sexually indeterminate Doppelgänger of the heterosexual leading man. Sexually obsessed and/or sexually indeterminate (the beginning of a long campaign by the cinema to demonize gays, lesbians, and racial minorities), "heavies" drank to excess, used drugs, treated women as mere chattel, were prone to violence, and were cowardly, weak, lazy, infantile. They were the inverse image of their more desirable screen counterparts. Walter Long and silent actor James Mason (not to be confused with the British screen actor of the late 1940s to mid 1980s, who also projected an aura of menace and sadism in many of his roles) were early archetypes of this curious figure, an immediately identifiable icon whose mere presence signaled peril for both the hero and the heroine. Often he was unkempt, unwashed, unshaven, and had missing teeth; he was exclusively male. In every way, the villain of the silent screen epitomized, as he still does, the generic instant-read icon of heterosexuality in ruins, the result of decadency, decay, and debauchery. Women villains were almost invariably vamps, epitomized by Theda Bara (born

Theodosia Goodman). The vamp was hypersexualized, constantly on the prowl for men to bring to ruin—old men (if they were wealthy), young men (if they were superficially attractive), or any man (if the mood struck the vamp, any heterosexual man was fair game, for revenge, sport, or mere recreation). Curiously, the only defense of the heterosexual male from the vamp was an absolute absence of desire; gay men were safe from her predatory advances, as were lesbians (although this subject was, naturally, never directly mentioned). Mary Pickford and her cinematic competitors offered the image of unattainable purity to their devoted swains, with sexual intimacy a complete impossibility. Theda Bara, Louise Glaum, Virginia Pearson, Barbara LaMarr, and Valeska Suratt offered the promise of sexual license to men (who were understandably frustrated by the unrealistic construct of the Mary Pickford alternative), but at a price: financial and moral ruin, the disapproval of conventional society, a sexual aggressor whose embrace signaled moral oblivion.

To offset this gallery of unrealistic heterocentric figures, the movies offered a series of comic types. They offered qualified relief from the moral constraints of genre casting. Freed from the burden of sexual attraction, women and men alike found a certain freedom in the comic personae who mocked the conventions of heterosexual screen desire while simultaneously strengthening its hold on the popular imagination through burlesque: Ben Turpin, with his perpetually crossed eyes; Slim Summerville, another rural caricature, whose career extended well into the era of sound films; Mack Swain, Oliver Hardy (before his teaming with Stan Laurel), and Fatty Arbuckle, rotund comedians who played frustrated suitors or villains with surprising interchangeability; Polly Moran and Louise Fazenda, forerunners of the comic sexual predator (later to be portrayed by Martha Raye, Cass Daley, and other women who abandoned the conventional trappings of cinematic femininity to create grotesque, comic foils for the equally inept and conventionally undesirable swains).

Serials came into prominence, and they offered women a bizarre alternative to the golden-haired, artificial purity of the early screen ingénue. Kathlyn Williams, who also directed some of her films, pioneered this new genre of constant action, peril, and unremitting physicality in the multichapter *Adventures of Kathlyn* (1913). Partnered with the new "serial queens," women of resourcefulness and daring, were a new breed of action heroes. They plunged furiously through episode after episode, intent upon aiding the heroine in her quest to unmask the mystery villain, who was usually revealed to be a respected member of the community, ostensibly above suspicion. Plots were secondary to the main requirement of the serial format: constant action, with the protagonists escaping one moment of disaster only to be faced with another dire predicament almost immediately. In such a hectic setting, romance was out of the question, or it was confined to a quick kiss as either the hero or the heroine embarked upon a particularly dangerous exploit.

The serial format, with its complete absence of characterization and utter reliance upon spectacle and violence to sustain audience interest, has arguably proven to be the cinema's most commercially durable genre. More recent films such as *Star Wars* (1977), *Raiders of the Lost Ark* (1981), *The Mummy* (1999), and their subsequent sequels are merely feature-length versions of serials, with each successive sequel portraying another chapter of the ongoing struggle. As with the early serials, these contemporary cliffhangers employ a variety of tie-ins to maximize audience interest. In the day of *The Adventures of Kathlyn,* there were only newspaper tie-ins to turn to; today, distributors have television, radio, the Internet, cable television, VHS tapes, DVDs, and a host of ancillary media, including print, to exploit their wares.

For all their thematic shortcomings, serials did offer women a more desirable role within the heterosexualized embrace of the dominant sphere. Instead of being acted upon, women in serials were themselves figures of action; they often rescued the putative hero from danger at the last possible moment. In their self-reliance, determination, stamina, and self-esteem, such early serial heroines as Florence La Badie, Mary Fuller, Marguerite Snow, Natalie Kingston, Ethel Grandin, Ruth Roland, Helen Greene, Pearl White, and Anne Luther prefigured the self-reliant "Hawksian woman" of the early 1930s to late 1960s. These women were not waiting to be rescued by anyone; they took matters into their own hands. Significantly, many of these early serial queens, especially Pearl White and Ruth Roland, also insisted upon doing their own stunts, thus adding another dimension of risk and danger to the films in which they appeared.

Bronco Billy Anderson (Gilbert M. Anderson in real life) was the screen's first cowboy hero. Anderson's early westerns were undistinguished and failed to capture the public's attention because, as Anderson later admitted, they lacked a central character with whom the audience could identify. In addition, Anderson was a victim of the Edison trust's vindictiveness and was forced to move to California in the early part of 1907 to escape a flurry of lawsuits. The first Broncho Billy western was *The Bandit Makes Good* (1907), which Anderson directed and in which he starred. The Broncho Billy character was an impossible and implausible amalgam of strength, virtue, bashfulness, and heroism—as were other early screen heroes—and the plot for each new Broncho Billy western was the same. Pitted against a motley variety of dastardly villains who sought to besmirch the heroine's virtue, purloin her savings, and/or steal the family homestead, Broncho Billy would undergo the expected difficulties required of the genre and inevitably triumph; he would win the heart of the heroine, the gratitude of her parents, and the devotion of millions of screen admirers. Between 1907 and 1914, Anderson cranked out nearly four hundred Broncho Billy westerns. He starred in and directed all of them, and became one of the screen's first and most successful actor-directors, the forerunner of figures such as Clint Eastwood and Warren Beatty.

As Broncho Billy's career expired, a newer, more brutal western star appeared on the horizon, one who would make the theatrical antics of Anderson's creation seem quaintly outdated. If early westerns were stagy and unrealistic, the films of William S. Hart brought a new dimension of violence and brutality to the screen; audiences immediately responded. Hart picked up much of the character he would later portray in his films while working as a ranch hand. Hart's penchant for violent realism was echoed in other then-contemporary westerns. Nowhere was the new code of the West more explicitly portrayed than in the numerous fight scenes that punctuated the westerns in the latter part of the silent era.

Violence in film had become entirely pervasive. The 1914 western *The Spoilers* features a classic fight scene that lasted nearly ten minutes and established a new benchmark for screen violence. *The Spoilers* was remade three times, in 1923, 1930, and 1942, but the original with Tom Santschi and William Farnum remains the standard by which all the sequels were judged (if only because in the 1914 version Farnum and Santschi eschewed the use of stunt doubles). As the serials offered an unceasing spectacle of violence and destruction, westerns and other genre films increasingly came to rely on action sequences, especially scenes involving hand-to-hand conflict, to keep audiences entertained. Just as chase sequences in *Bullitt* (1968), *The French Connection* (1971), and *The Seven-Ups* (1973) all attempted to best each other in excess of speed and motion, so too did violence, particularly between heterosexual males, become a station of the cross in narrative genre cinema. Thus was the screen fight as a test of manhood created, in such films as *Lone Hand Saunders* (1926), *The Sea Beast* (1926, starring John Barrymore), and *The Black Pirate* (1926, starring Douglas Fairbanks, Sr.). Whether trying to push someone off a building or ship or into a smoldering geyser (Griffith and Mayer 100–01) or fending off an unequal mob with studied nonchalance, the silent screen heterosexual male had to prove himself primarily through his fists—as well as through his carefully circumscribed ardor toward the film's nominal heroine. In the silent era, such violent spectacles of manhood were accompanied by performative displays of heterotopic affection. By the late 1990s, with the risk of HIV/AIDS making sexuality both dangerous and problematic, these ritualized scenes of intimate physical violence had largely *replaced* scenes of heterosexual coupling in the dominant Hollywood cinema. Violence became the sole content of much of the mainstream cinema, as the romantic surtext was stripped away to reveal a contested site of corporeal disease.

During this period of cinematic history, roughly between 1894 and 1920, the basic characteristics of the leading man were rigidly encoded into the cinematic matrix: facial type (conventionally featured, white, Anglo-Saxon); hair (blond or brown, straight and smooth); height (between five feet eight inches and six feet tall, with minor exceptions; the exceptions used lifts or apple boxes to achieve the required measurement); weight (slim, flat chested, yet robust and muscular); clothing (entirely a function of the genre, but whether an action film or a drawing-room comedy, the hero's clothing always remained immaculate); and overall demeanor (kind, considerate, slow to anger, quick to redress a wrong, just, chaste, and attracted only to heterosexual women of his own social class). This utterly unreal masculine composite was matched by his equally manufactured female counterpart, the heroine who was usually blond, mild mannered, endlessly deferential, Anglo-Saxon, with even features, about five feet four inches in height, fashionably slim, dressed to be simultaneously attractive yet not obviously forward, and seeking nothing more than the artificial splendor of a lifetime heterosexual marital contract, in which both partners would cohabitate in a state of semicelibate suspended animation.

The plasticity of these constructs has never really been questioned, even in contemporary cinema, and the pernicious hold of these racist, colonialist, and sexist stereotypes has become, if anything, more rigidly encoded today. In *The Mummy Returns,* Rick O'Connell (Brendan Fraser) is the stalwart, slightly dumb hero who stumbles from one breakneck adventure to another; Evelyn Carnahan O'Connell (Rachel Weisz), is his adoring wife (who, in a perfunctory nod to feminism, is allowed to engage in some hand-to-hand combat with the film's vamp, Anck-Su-Namun [Patricia Velazquez], mistress to Im-Ho-Tep [Arnold Vosloo]). Tagging along for the ride is their adorable eight-year-old son, Alex (Freddie Boath), who along with his mother is periodically abducted so that they can be heroically rescued in subsequent scenes. Evelyn's brother, Jonathan (John Hannah), is the stiff-upper-lip comic-relief British aristocrat whose miscalculations continually bring misfortune to the group, and Ardeth Bay (Oded Fehr) serves as the tribal leader of a group of colonized native subjects whose sole purpose within the film's narrative is to assist Rick, Evelyn, and Alex. While Im-Ho-Tep, the Mummy, is the film's putative villain, the final confrontation is between Rick and the Scorpion King (Dwayne Johnson, aka "The Rock"), who through the use of extensive digital effects is transformed into a half-man–half-scorpion monstrosity in a final, predicable battle to the death. All of this takes place in the comfortably colonialist past of 1933. We are never allowed for a moment to question why three Caucasians form the focus of the film's narrative, never allowed to wonder why all the minorities in the film, with the exception of Ardeth Bay and his tribesmen, are irredeemably evil, bent only upon domination, destruction, and violence. The film continually advances England as the guardian of "civilization" (although this conservatorship seems confined to the developed space of the British Museum where, appropriately, Im-Ho-Tep is reincarnated yet again to fight against the forces of the empire).

The cardboard characterizations in *The Mummy Returns* are redolent of silent serials, and the heterosexually based embrace of the family unit above all other social formations echoes the tropes created by Griffith, Edison, and Porter. The unbridled racism of the film and the celebration of the construct of whiteness as the dominant narrative linchpin of the film's value system are equaled only by the rigidly circumscribed sexual roles each character is called upon to signify. Rick is dashing, somewhat dim, and conventionally handsome; Evelyn can kick ass when the occasion demands it but is much more comfortable as a nurturing mother; Alex is a representative of the impossibly spoiled youth of the aristocracy, endlessly mischievous, yet—at eight—enough of a scholar to read cuneiform on sight. Jonathan, Evelyn's brother, is entirely sexless; his neutered state befits his positioning as the film's perennial sidekick. Lock-Nah (Adewale Akinnuoye-Agbaje) and the rest of Im-Ho-Tep's and the Scorpion King's allies, suitably othered, also fit comfortably within the screenplay's good guy–bad guy, good girl–bad girl mentality. Not only is there absolutely nothing original in all of this, but the film represents a pernicious return to the stereotypically heterosexual, colonial fantasies of the Victorian era. Perhaps it is for this reason that it has enjoyed massive success at the box office. As a return to the past, the film substitutes the wearying procession of one digital effect after another in the place of a narrative (as did Méliès's shorter, more inventive films a century earlier) and ensures that no sexual ambiguity is allowed to seep through the cracks of the film's carefully encoded sexual stereotypes. The protagonists of *The Mummy Returns,* not so much characters as narrative positionings, are trapped in a world of colonialist social and sexual repression. It is reminiscent of *The Four Feathers* (1939), the hypercolonialist film based on A. E. W. Mason's story of a disgraced army officer who must prove himself to his colleagues after faltering in battle. Significantly, *The Four Feathers* has also recently been excavated from the vaults for a remake, and perhaps even the most casual viewer of these films can perceive that this is more than mere coincidence. Trapped in a world that demands constant proof of their heterosexuality and will to fight, the characters in *The Mummy Returns* sleepwalk through the mayhem that surrounds them with a confidence borne of a century of generic cinematic discourse. White makes right; minorities are marginalized; only violence helps where violence rules; the heterocentric mythos remains at the center of the cinema.

CHAPTER TWO

Breaks in the System

But cracks started to appear in the rigid structure of the heterocentric cinema even as it was being invented. In 1895, Edison and his associate W. K. L. Dickson photographed an experimental sound film, which historian Vito Russo identifies in *The Celluloid Closet* as *The Gay Brothers* (6, 7). However, the title seems apocryphal, for Edison himself titled the project *Dickson Experimental Sound Film,* or *Dickson Violin.* The film shows two men dancing a sort of waltz while another Edison employee, Charles D'Almaine, plays the violin as accompaniment (Musser 178). However, I would argue that the film, far from being a projection (in every sense of the word) of homosexuality into the cinema, instead portrays a more confidently relaxed attitude toward heterosexuality during the era; it was a time when two men could dance together without arousing comment. In the same fashion, early drag film appearances by John Bunny, Wallace Beery, Fatty Arbuckle, Charles Chaplin, Stan Laurel (Russo 8–10), and others constituted carefully timed acts of social disruption, yet even as they burlesqued the construction of sexual identities, these performers also buttressed them. None of the drag performances were convincing, and all were engineered for maximum comic effect.

The real fissures in dominant cinema ideology appeared when gay and bisexual actors were forced by the increasing rigidity of social convention to adopt straight personae for the screen.

> Heterosexuals entered the world of film through clearly marked doors. There were inspiring heroes or heroines for them to identify with. Even the unheroic could identify with popular character players, but homosexuals hit a yellow brick wall. We simply did not exist.
>
> Other minorities had films from their native lands, however few, or Hollywood images, however artificial, providing images, however limiting, in stories, however hypocritical, that promised them advancement, however conformist. They longed to pass. Homosexuals had to. (Patrick 11)

After the 1925 version of *Ben-Hur,* Ramon Novarro's career went into steep decline because he refused to conform to the heterosexual screen image his studio demanded (Hadleigh, *Lavender* 13). Alla Nazimova was relegated to the margins of cinematic discourse when her lesbianism became public knowledge (Russo 27). Rock Hudson's performative heterosexual display fooled audiences for a quarter of a century, but the pity of this masquerade is that he was forced into it by the circumstances and prejudices of the era, prejudices that survive today. Hudson's posthumous autobiography, in which the actor for the first time disclosed that he was gay, was one of the first signs that, at last, the wall of silence surrounding performative heterosexuality was crumbling. Marlene Dietrich, Anthony Perkins, Greta Garbo, Charles Laughton, Tallulah Bankhead, Cesar Romero, Barbara Stanwyck, Cary Grant, and Joan Crawford (to name just a few prominent actors) were all bisexual or homosexual, but they kept their sexual orientation secret for fear of alienating their fans (see Hadleigh, *Hollywood Gays;* Russo; Cawthorne; and Ehrenstein for a fuller discussion of this sad American cultural phenomenon). When Anne Heche came out as Ellen DeGeneres's lover, Hollywood professionals questioned whether the public would accept her as Harrison Ford's love interest in the heterocentric screwball comedy *Six Days, Seven Nights* (1998). For whatever reason, the film did only middling business at the box office, adding no luster to Heche's career, and Ellen DeGeneres's sitcom, *Ellen,* was soon canceled. Perhaps not surprisingly, Heche and DeGeneres ultimately split up as a couple, and Heche subsequently became involved in a highly publicized heterosexual relationship. DeGeneres, meanwhile, was given another shot at a sitcom in the fall of 2001.

As Eve Kosofsky Sedgwick remarks, "Even at an individual level, there are remarkably few of even the most openly gay people who are not deliberately in the closet with someone personally or economically or institutionally important to them" (67–68). As we enter a new century of film development, we are still clinging to the construction of straight relationships with as much urgency as we did in the movies' infancy. Will we ever move beyond this state of performative stasis? The evidence suggests that we have become all too comfortable with the normative vision of straight performed heterosexuality in the cinema and that, for the present—despite efforts from the margins to undermine and transmogrify the existing commodification of heterosexually based filmic values—these century-old figures and role positionings will continue to dominate the commercial discourse of cinema for some time to come.

Allied with this need to "normalize" sexual behavior into a rigidly defined code of behavior is a desire to exile all potentially disruptive forms of social discourse, or at least to contain them within the boundaries of a carefully designed series of sexual and performative tropes. In addition, the exoticization and othering of all non-American, non-Caucasian cultures by dominant Hollywood cinema practice continues to ensure cultural and social marginalization for most of the world's inhabitants. In his groundbreaking study *White,* Richard Dyer notes,

> All concepts of race are always concepts of the body and also of heterosexuality. Race is a means of categorising different types of human body which reproduce themselves. It seeks to systematise differences and to relate them to differences of character and worth. Heterosexuality is the means of ensuring, but also the site of endangering, the reproduction of these differences. (20)

Thus it is not enough to create a white, heterocentric universe and people it with artificially created constructs to bring it to life. One must also create a perpetual underclass, a racial and sexual divide that cannot be grudged, and then construct human exemplars to people this phantom universe. In the early days of the cinema, no "location" captured the imagination of popular mythmakers more than the epistemological territory of the jungle, with its lush undergrowth and hidden grottoes obscuring the inhabitants from public view. Almost immediately, the Hollywood film machine turned its attention to Africa as the primal location of the other. Hollywood sought to exoticize, differentiate, and colonialize African social practice and culture into the most visible example of this demimonde. Martin and Osa Johnson, a husband-and-wife team of "explorers," were among the first to bring this new racializing, othering spectacle before the public. Their films were titled *Cannibals of the South Seas* (1912), *Jungle Adventures* (1921), *Head Hunters of the South Seas* (1922), and *Trailing African Wild Animals* (1923).

Even more constructed are such exoticizing films as *Virgins of Bali* (1932), designed solely "to flaunt the bodies of a pair of beautiful Balinese teenagers" (Doherty, *Pre-Code* 234), and the spectacularly fraudulent *Ingagi* (1930), a completely faked jungle film. *Ingagi* was supposedly shot in the "darkness" of Africa but was in fact composed of a plethora of staged footage shot in California, hastily and sloppily intercut with material from the 1914 documentary *The Heart of Africa* (236–41). An MGM house director, W. S. Van Dyke, who later created *Eskimo* (1933) using a combination of location and studio footage, also created perhaps the most ambitious African "safari film" of the period, *Trader Horn* (1931). Van Dyke was something of an expert at manufactured exoticism, having taken over the direction of *White Shadows in the South Seas* (1928) on location in Tahiti for Robert Flaherty (creator of the stage-managed "documentaries" *Nanook of the North* [1922] and *Moana* [1926]). Van Dyke originally signed on as Flaherty's assistant, but Flaherty was unable to reconcile himself with the creation of a *wholly* fictional narrative using native actors—although he had been perfectly willing to recreate and simulate much of the material in *Nanook* and *Moana,* both of which were publicized as "pure" documentaries (Cannom 159–72). Van Dyke took over the production of *White Shadows* and brought it in on time, even ahead of schedule; in it he emphasized the more exotic and sensual aspects of the material. *White Shadows in the South Seas* proved a great success when released with music and sound effects by MGM, and almost immediately Van Dyke found himself typed as the studio's foremost expert in cinematic exoticism. In February 1929, Van Dyke's camera crew went to Africa and shot 450,000 feet of 35mm film on location (Cannom 227), but upon his return, the studio decided to photograph additional material in Mexico to cover up technical gaffes, improve sound quality, and allow for slicker, studio-quality close-ups of the principal actors. What emerged was the template for the jungle film that became a popular subgenre, lasting well into the present era. *Trader Horn* tells the story of a lost white princess (Edwina Booth) and her return to "civilization" under the auspices of white hunter Trader Horn (Harry Carey) and his assistant, played by Duncan Renaldo. This material would be recycled, both thematically and physically, for several decades.

Other films that sought to enhance the cultural supremacy of America at the expense of other cultures during this period include *Explorers of the World* (1931), a compilation film of various ethnographers roaming the globe; *With Byrd at the South Pole* (1930), which displayed the vast frozen wastes of Antarctica as a trophy for paying customers; *Igloo* (1932); and *S.O.S. Iceberg* (1933; Doherty, *Pre-Code* 227–29). The practice of putting foreign cultures on display as curiosities extended as well to James A. Fitzpatrick's *Traveltalks,* a long-running series of one-reel films for MGM that dealt, for the most part, with travel to European, Asian, and Middle Eastern nations and colonial outposts of the various empire nations in Africa and the Far East. When Fitzpatrick ventured into the United States with his early three-strip Technicolor camera crew, he portrayed American society as an unending marvel of architectural and social ingenuity; but when he ventured outside North America, Fitzpatrick's narration consistently exoticized the cultures he ostensibly sought to document.

Frank Buck created a brutal series of staged ethnographic films, beginning with *Bring 'Em Back Alive* (1932) and continuing with *Wild Cargo* (1934). The films presented staged battles between leopards, pythons, tigers, crocodiles, and other indigenous wildlife with little regard for authenticity (Doherty, *Pre-Code* 243–45). Yet for all the fakery in these pseudo-ethnographic films, one element was not falsified: death. Many of the animals forced to take part in the inequitable battles staged by Buck and his confederates died. As in the *Faces of Death* series, what is being conveyed by Fitzpatrick is nothing less than violent death for spectatorial pleasure—the totemic equivalent of the snuff film.

No matter where the makers of these films, feature length or short subject, chose to place their cameras, and no matter what their approach to the material at hand (frankly exploitational and sensationalistic or a more relaxed travelogue, with scenes of buildings and street celebrations parading across the screen in front of the presumably mesmerized viewer), the underlying subtext was always the same.

Whatever the nominal cover story for the expeditionary film (a fight for survival against uncaring Nature, a Romeo and Juliet romance in tribal dress) and whoever the star native (the great hunter, the struggling farmer, the beautiful maiden), the real story is always: Great White Photographer Brings Back Movies from Savage Land for American Moviegoers. (Doherty, *Pre-Code* 226)

The trend toward staged "ethnography" was also exemplified by *Frozen Justice* (1929), featuring Lenore Ulric as an Eskimo vamp, as well as *Mount McKinley* (1924), *Beau Sabreur* (1928), *Gateway of the Moon* (1928), *Hula* (1927), *Tabu* (1931), and *Aloma of the South Seas* (1926). All of these, to varying degrees, combined staged narratives with genuine or fraudulent location footage to create a desert epic, a trip to the South Seas, or a visit to the frozen north (Griffith and Mayer 106–09). The classic studio film also conflated foreignness with increased heterosexual desire not only in the frankly exploitational films *Ingagi* and *Virgins of Bali,* but in such back-lot fantasies as *Paris in Spring* (1935), *Paris at Midnight* (1926), *Paris Honeymoon* (1939), *Paris Interlude* (1934), and numerous other films. These equated anything foreign with mystery, intrigue, and a sexual license that was unthinkable within the bounds of white, heterosexual American society.

If France fostered an atmosphere of devil-may-care decadence in the minds of the average American filmgoer, China, Japan, and other Eastern locales inevitably brought forth visions of opium dens, exotic temptresses, and torture by various unusual methods. Novelist Sax Rohmer's fictional Dr. Fu Manchu became the most notorious figurehead for these xenophobic fantasies. (In them, paradoxically, such British colonial stalwarts as Boris Karloff portrayed Fu Manchu in "race" drag, while his minions remained [for the most part] authentically Asian.) The commercial success of the Fu Manchu series ensured the longevity of the odious subgenre of "yellow-peril" films, which have, amazingly, lasted from the silent era until the present day (although the racism has become, in time, more subtly encoded). Such peculiar films as *Confessions of an Opium Eater* (1962)—in which Vincent Price wanders through San Francisco's Chinatown in the nineteenth century in an opium-induced daze—or the Hammer studio's series of Fu Manchu films in the 1960s, with Christopher Lee, demonstrate conclusively that racist social constructs do not disappear with the passage of time but are merely camouflaged with a revised set of cultural signifiers.

Yet America was not portrayed as an entirely heterogeneous whole; even within the dominion itself there were cultural conflicts between urban and rural lifestyles. These were sometimes used cinematically for comic effect, and sometimes to erect barriers between various portions of the population. African Americans were, of course, the most brutally segmented portion of the population. They were reduced to playing bootblacks and porters in the dominant cinema, even as they created an alternate vision of their own in the inevitably impoverished films of Oscar Micheaux and Spencer Williams. More subtle, however, was the gap between the classes, delineated not only by income but also by accidents of birth and education. In *The Girl Who Ran Wild* (1922) and *Tol'able David* (first made in 1921 and remade in 1930), rural America is seen as a hellhole of inbreeding, cruelty, and violence, with alcoholism and poverty ever present features of the social landscape. Marginal pockets of American society—circus performers, truckdrivers, drifters, criminals, and the physically deformed and mentally challenged—were all portrayed as living a different sort of life from that of the average American, a life fraught with both danger and temptation. Homosexuals, especially, were singled out for ridicule. It was insulting enough that lesbian and gay actors were forced to heterosexualize themselves to pass muster with their employers and admirers. But when homosexuality *was* portrayed on the screen, it was almost invariably cast in an unflattering light. In much the same manner, women who dared to be independent were suspect. Marlene Dietrich might kiss a woman on the lips with casual insouciance as a throwaway gesture in *Morocco* (1930), but this isolated instance of sexual performative freedom was counterbalanced by a veritable avalanche of insulting sexual stereotypes. Edward Everett Horton, Eric Blore, Franklin Pangborn, Grady Sutton, George K. Arthur, and other supporting performers were employed with stunning regularity to bring to life a gallery of "sissies" and "pansies" in films of the 1930s and 1940s (Russo 30–39). Gay stereotypes also pervade cartoons of the early 1930s; in *Betty Boop's Penthouse* (1933), a newly created Frankensteinesque monster is rendered harmless with a few sprays of "Eau de Pansy" and is transformed from a hulking brute into a sensuously rotoscoped ballet dancer. In Clara Bow's comeback vehicle, the rather amazing *Call Her Savage* (1932), Clara and her escort visit a gay bar in Greenwich Village, which has been described as existing "down in the village where only wild poets and anarchists are. It's pretty rough" (qtd. in Russo 42). The club itself, however, is a rather tame, if smoky, establishment filled with cartoonish bearded revolutionaries and artists, the only people willing to tolerate the other patrons of the club, who are pairs of neatly dressed men and slightly tweedy women sitting in booths with their arms draped around each other. . . . In the aisles, two willowy young men in frilly white aprons and maid's caps are performing a musical number. Each carries a feather duster, a prop for the song in progress. The lyrics erase any doubt about the sexuality of characters who for years were "just sissies."

> If a sailor in pajamas I should see
> I know he'll scare the life out of me
> But on a great big battleship
> *(Together)* We'd like to be
> Working as chamber maids! (Russo 42–43)

Lesbianism was seen as equally threatening. In the film *The Warrior's Husband* (1933) and the science-fiction fantasy *Just Imagine* (1930), viewers are shown a glimpse of a world in which a lesbian matriarchy rules in place of the usual governing body of heterosexual males (Russo 39).

As the late 1920s crashed into the grim Great Depression–era 1930s, audiences were eager for anything that diverged from normative values. Between 1930 and 1934, before the Hays-Breen office enforced the Motion Picture Production Code, viewers had an opportunity vicariously to walk on the wild side. In *Baby Face* (1933), Barbara Stanwyck slept her way to the top of the business world with cool calculation and no regrets. In *The Story of Temple Drake* (1933), based on William Faulkner's novel *Sanctuary*, Miriam Hopkins plays an heiress who is kidnapped and then raped by perennial heavy Jack La Rue (this film was too much even for the more liberal members of the press and was reviled by reviewers even before its release). Mae West created a comic, yet curiously touching figure of heterosexual female desire in her pre-Code classics *She Done Him Wrong* (1933) and *I'm No Angel* (1933). When the Code censored her delicious double-entendre dialogue, much of which West wrote herself, her career went into a decline from which it never truly recovered. *Red Dust* (1932) offered Jean Harlow as a Saigon prostitute falling in love with Clark Gable over the objections of good-girl Mary Astor. *Safe in Hell* (1931) shows Dorothy Mackaill stuck in a tropic hell from which society will not allow her to escape, as a particularly seedy and rapacious group of "suitors" anticipate her next move. *Red Headed Woman* (1932), one of the most brazen of the pre-Code films, offers viewers the spectacle of Harlow dying her hair red, in defiance of her platinum-blond screen image, and then launching on an energetic campaign to snare (and bankrupt) as many men as she possibly can. The film ends with Harlow still living the lush life, despite some inevitable reversals along the way. *Three on a Match* (1932) presents, in little over an hour, the encapsulated lives of three women (played by Bette Davis, Ann Dvorak, and Joan Blondell) who accidentally meet again as adults after going their separate ways in childhood. Dvorak's character, married to an attorney played by Warren William, is rich and bored and soon finds excitement of a sort with a gambler played by Lyle Talbot. In short order, Dvorak's character becomes an alcoholic cocaine addict who spirals down to kidnapping and suicide by the film's end. *Shanghai Express* (1932) offers Anna May Wong and Marlene Dietrich as women competing for the affections of Clive Brook's character. They are all aboard a train traveling through a phantasmagorical vision of China. *Heat Lighting* (1934) presents Aline MacMahon as Olga, a woman who owns a gas station–motel in the middle of the desert; she has been disappointed in love and wants to withdraw from the world. Ann Dvorak, playing Olga's younger sister, Myra, dreams of travel to exotic places but is instead the victim of date rape. When Olga's criminal ex-lover appears, Olga momentarily softens (much to her later regret) but, regaining her composure, she shoots him dead when he again betrays her. The authorities implicitly agree to a cover-up of the murder. *She Had to Say Yes* (1933) features Loretta Young as a secretary for a clothing firm that uses "customer's girls" (read *prostitutes*) to lure potential buyers; when times get too tough, the secretary's boyfriend urges her to "entertain" clients as well. In all of these films, the vision of life portrayed is anything but the heterosexually based bliss that became the American cinema's sole stock in trade after 1934, when Shirley Temple became the hottest box-office star in Hollywood. What these films present is a world shorn of decency, hope, and faith, a world in which sheer economic necessity drives people to sell themselves to the highest bidder.

What sort of vision of heterosexuality do these films offer? In pre-Code productions, sex was either a liability or an asset, something to be trafficked and bartered. Men exploited women, and women used men to get what they wanted or needed—food, clothing, a place to sleep. Sex became a commodity rather than a celebratory or procreative act. At the same time, the safety of the heterocentric family unit crumbled. In *Wild Boys of the Road* (1933), the character played by Frankie Darro hit the road with his teenage pals when they discover that their parents can no longer afford to support them. They endure lives of hardship and unremitting violence, which starkly contrast the world of Saturday dances and family dinners they have been forced to abandon. The fabric of society itself was becoming worn and frayed. *The Dark Horse* (1932) and *The Phantom President* (1932) ridicule not only politicians but also the voters who put them in office; both movies depict office seekers as self-aggrandizing egomaniacs who care only about their own advancement. In *The Mouthpiece* (1932), Warren William railroads an innocent man to the electric chair and, in shock and remorse, decides to represent the lowest criminal element of society. He then wins freedom for a series of murderers, hoodlums, and thugs as he thumbs his nose at the conventional standard of justice. *Five Star Final* (1931) offers Edward G. Robinson as the editor of a notorious New York tabloid (loosely modeled on the notorious New York *Graphic*). He resurrects a decades-old scandal to increase circulation, and drives a couple to suicide in the process. Nothing is too venal for the reporters on this fictional paper: Boris Karloff poses as a priest to extract information from the unsuspecting victims, while later, photographers break into the couple's apartment to obtain exclusive photographs of their suicide. *American Madness* (1932), an early Frank Capra film, presents a much darker view of the world than that shown in his later populist confections. *American Madness* depicts the banking business essentially as a racket, in which honesty and fair play have no part. Indeed, *Love Is a Racket* (1932), *Beauty for Sale* (1932), *Heroes for Sale* (1933), *I Am a Fugitive from a Chain Gang* (1932), *Okay, America* (1932), and other early 1930s films depict a world devoid of hope, in which the populace is divided between hucksters and victims. People survive as best they can, or they do not survive at all.

These films signaled the collapse of American confidence in government, the press, and the fabric of heterosexual family life. What was the point of marrying and having children when the world was such a compromised and unforgiving domain? And yet this rupture in the fabric of heterocentric social existence had been building for several decades; by the time it flooded out onto the screen in an explosion of despair, the public was ready for any ideal, any ideological construct that would restore hope to their lives. Thus was born Shirley Temple, usually depicted as an orphan or a lost child, doggedly seeking to reestablish a family unit in the midst of war or personal misfortune. The wave of phantasmal, artificially cheerful films that followed—including *Little Women* (1933), *Little Lord Fauntleroy* (1936), *When a Feller Needs a Friend* (1932), *Penrod and Sam* (1937), and the Andy Hardy series—demonstrates that Hollywood was now desperate to restore confidence in a heteronormative system of values that had been seen as bankrupt only months before. The speed of the reversal and the depth of the repressive forces at work are amazing. Essentially, the cinema never really recovered from the effects of the Code's enactment because the basic cycle of cinematic freedom and then restraint had been established. Periods of social experimentation were followed by decades of retrenchment, so that the 1920s and the 1960s stand out within the century's social and cinematic discourse as isolated zones of personal expression, adrift in a landscape of carefully stage managed social engineering, in which business interests were allowed to dominate all other forms of human endeavor.

By the time the pre-Code films collapsed in a haze of forced heterosexual performativity in the mid 1930s, the basic, generic pattern for the marriage contract, the courting ritual, and the supposed polarity between men and women in the cinema had been established. The straight world was seen as encompassing all social commerce, and all exceptions were ruthlessly marginalized. In World War I, the threat of invasion served as the impetus for heterosexual union in *War Brides* (1916) with real-life lesbian Alla Nazimova offering herself to the gods of heterosexism as a sacrifice to the war effort. Simultaneously, heterotopia was under fire from benign neglect in *The Fall of a Nation* (1916), a filmic narrative "exploring" the dangers of pacifism. Absence and mourning were depicted on the home front in *The Service Star* (1918), starring Madge Kennedy as a mother whose son serves in combat duty overseas. The films of Cecil B. DeMille offered heterosexual desire in the domain of the spectacle, conflating sexual desire with fleshly corruption but holding out the promise of redemption for the last reel. In DeMille's 1915 *The Cheat,* a supposedly virtuous woman feigns the role of a seducer in service of the narrative, thus setting up a dialectical confrontation between desire and abstinence, failure and triumph, sanctity and figurative damnation. Other DeMille films, including *Male and Female* (1919), *Saturday Night* (1922), *The Golden Bed* (1925), *Why Change Your Wife?* (1920), and *The Sign of the Cross* (1932), pushed DeMille's penchant for melodramatic and narrativistic excess to new heights while simultaneously positing the dangers of excess in marital and extramarital social and sexual intercourse.

The 1920s also witnessed changing heterosexual styles of screen romance, with the ascension of Rudolph Valentino in *The Sheik* (1921), *The Four Horsemen of the Apocalypse* (1921), and *A Sainted Devil* (1924). Following in Valentino's wake were other "exotic" (read *Latino*) purveyors of forbidden masculine desire, actors such as Ramon Novarro and Ricardo Cortez, who paved the way for contemporary stars like Antonio Banderas. Romance was still conducted according to rules and regulations. Elinor Glyn's novel *Three Weeks* was the 1920s version of *The Rules* and was transformed into a spectacular paean to conventionalized heterosexual romance in 1924. This formula was also followed by *Paid to Love* (1927), *The Prisoner of Zenda* (1922, 1937, and subsequent versions), *Love's Blindness* (1926), *His Hour* (1924), and other fabulist's tales of heterosexualized romance. These utopian visions of the heterosexual congress were followed by cautionary confessional romances in which purity triumphs over momentary temptation, as in *Three Sinners* (1928), *Happiness Ahead* (1928), and *The Man Who Fights Alone* (1924).

A series of social ruptures in late-1920s Hollywood further solidified the hold of the heterocentric vision on the public. The scandals surrounding the death of Virginia Rappe at a party given by Roscoe "Fatty" Arbuckle, the murder of William Desmond Taylor, and the drug-overdose death of "handsome" Wallace Reid (husband of Dorothy Davenport Reid, as previously noted), made the public feel as if Hollywood was nothing more than a sewer of sin and fleshly corruption. This gave rise to such religious epics as *The King of Kings* (1927), *Ben-Hur* (1925), and *The Ten Commandments* (1923) as harbingers of a new code of moral regulation and social and sexual restriction. Significantly, all these films would be remade in the late 1950s and early 1960s as a response to the perceived threat of communist influence in Hollywood.

Despite the swing to the right in the 1920s, such disruptive figures as Clara Bow, Alice White, and Louise Brooks were seen as icons of feminist determinacy, complemented nevertheless by their male heterosexual performative counterparts, Donald Keith, Eddie Philips, Malcolm McGregor, and Lawrence Gray. Films of this "new" moral standard included *Prodigal Daughters* (1923), *The Collegians* (1926), *The Plastic Age* (1925), and *Our Modern Maidens* (1929), an early vehicle for Joan Crawford. Wild parties, orgiastic excess, and images of transient pleasure also took center stage in *The Next Corner* (1924), *The Perfect Flapper* (1924), and other films of the period. As the twenties continued, Mae Murray, Mary

Pickford, Douglas Fairbanks, Sr., Corinne Griffith, Norma Talmadge, Lillian Gish, and Greta Garbo all rose to international prominence as iconic arbiters of heterosexual desire. The crushing, inescapable dominion of straight romance in cinema and American popular culture was most visualized by cinema's numerous love teams. Performed, visualized heterosexual desire was represented by such star pairings as Joseph Cotten and Jennifer Jones; Barbara Stanwyck and Robert Taylor; Fred Astaire and Ginger Rogers; Greta Garbo and John Gilbert; Vilma Banky and Ronald Colman; Janet Gaynor and Charles Farrell. These cinematic constructs further compartmentalized the domain of cinematic heterosexual desire.

With the onset of the Depression, the movie musical of the 1930s became a zone of corporeal dis-ease, in which Busby Berkeley fragmented the female body to create a series of dazzlingly kaleidoscopic yet dehumanized tableaux, while at RKO, Fred Astaire and Ginger Rogers offered a vaguely reassuring alternative: the idealized straight couple in danger of losing each other to outside interference (coded lesbians and gays, racially othered suitors, and other de-narrated threats) or the machinations of fate. The horror vogue of the early 1930s commingled sites of desire and destruction in *Dracula* (1931), *Frankenstein* (1931), *Dracula's Daughter* (1936, featuring the screen's first coded lesbian vampire), *The Invisible Man* (1933), and *The Mummy* (1932). (As with DeMille's biblical spectacles, these problematic configurations of ritualized heterosexual desire would be reworked in the repressive 1950s with an increase in explicit sex and/or violence to update the material for a newer, more jaded audience.) Other 1930s cycles included the gangster film (*Little Caesar* [1931], *The Public Enemy* [1931], *Scarface* [1932]), prefiguring the romance of violence evident in the later films of Anthony Mann and Sam Peckinpah; and tales of illicit romance, including *Back Street* (1932), *Possessed* (1931), and *Panama Flo* (1932), in which performed heterosexual desire rends the fabric of conventional social commerce.

After decades of roles in B westerns, John Wayne became a star in *Stagecoach* (1939). A new standard of straight, white, masculine stoicism was brought to the screen, and it lasted for the next twenty-five years. This misogynistic joint vision of Wayne and his mentor, the director John Ford, was countered by *Female* (1933) with Ruth Chatterton. Chatterton plays the female CEO of a large corporation, who, inverting the normative narratives of the era, uses and discards men during the course of business. In this variation of *She* (originally made in 1908; remade in 1911,

1916, 1917, 1925, 1935, 1965, and 2001, and the source for numerous filmic variants), crossed with *Ilsa, She Wolf of the SS* (1974; in the film's tag line Ilsa warns, "no man spends a night with me and lives!"), Chatterton's character intentionally sabotages the careers of all her heterosexual conquests until her ideal mate (played by George Brent) comes along. In the course of her campaign, Chatterton invites to her mansion a young man who is obviously homosexual; when the man displays no interest in seducing her, Chatterton rewards him with a trip to Europe and an education in the arts.

In contrast, the films of the late 1930s offered visions of heterosexualized idealization without risk or interplay. In films, Nelson Eddy and Jeanette MacDonald, Deanna Durbin, Shirley Temple, Grace Moore, Eleanor Powell, and Sonja Henie played sanitized heterosexual figures designed solely for display and consumption. They sing; they dance; they do everything except engage in an actual heterosexual relationship. The rise of screwball comedy in *It Happened One Night* (1934), *The Thin Man* (1934), and *My Man Godfrey* (1936)—to name just a few of the many possible examples—ushered in a new screen relationship between men and women: it presented a heterosexual relationship of equality and depth, within the context of the era, wherein men and women could be friends, as well as lovers. Courting rituals and romantic display in *Friends of Mr. Sweeney* (1934), *Bringing Up Baby* (1938), and *Nothing Sacred* (1937) gave audiences performative heterosexualized couples who seemingly abandoned their proscribed gender roles. Westerns became stylized zones of courtship with the bizarre singing-cowboy films of Gene Autry, Roy Rogers, and Dale Evans; in these films, heterosexual romance was enacted through a succession of musical numbers and antiseptic violence. The jungle film came into prominence in the many Tarzan films, beginning with *Tarzan, the Ape Man* (1932); the scant costumes of Johnny Weissmuller and Maureen O'Sullivan during several scenes of domestic interplay offered a glimpse of heterosexualized utopian desire to audiences in the 1930s and 1940s.

Yet the Hollywood cinema of the 1920s and 1930s was above all a racist and heterocentric construct, an all-white universe that allowed no roles of substance for African Americans or other minorities. In response, the all-black films of Oscar Micheaux, Spencer Williams, and others came into being, shot on shoestring budgets and released to all-black theaters. Titles include *The Symbol of the Unconquered* (1920); *Within Our Gates*

(1920); *The Blood of Jesus* (1941); *Body and Soul* (1924); *The Bronze Buckaroo* (1939); *The Duke Is Tops* (1938); *Miracle in Harlem* (1948); *Swing!* (1938); and *Song of Freedom* (1936). This last film was one of actor-singer-activist Paul Robeson's groundbreaking forays into the world of the dominant white Hollywood cinema.

As the Depression began to lift in the late 1930s, the threat and commencement of European war led to such films as *Mission to Moscow* (1943), *Confessions of a Nazi Spy* (1939), *Foreign Correspondent* (1940), and *Hitler's Children* (a 1943 film that featured a sequence depicting forced sterilization of German women "unfit" to give birth). The realm of performative heterosexualized desire was under attack from externalized forces. Wartime marriage and absence formed a new locus for male-female relationships in the 1940s, and the idealized early 1940s war film encapsulated patriotism, sacrifice, the sanctity of the idealized heterosexual couple, and Rosie the Riveter all in one highly conflicted series of narratives. Humphrey Bogart broke through the B film barrier into A films in *Casablanca* (1942) and *Action in the North Atlantic* (1943) as a new kind of male star, devoid of glamour but respected for his no-nonsense gruffness. Robert Mitchum, after numerous bit parts in Hop-Along Cassidy westerns, appeared in a brutal string of World War II action films, including *Gung Ho!* (1943) and *The Story of G. I. Joe* (1945). John Wayne starred in *The Sands of Iwo Jima* (1949), while escapist comedies (Olsen and Johnson, Abbott and Costello) alternated with patriotic and decidedly straight musicals (*Yankee Doodle Dandy* [1942], *This Is the Army* [1943], *Stage Door Canteen* [1943]) in an attempt to preserve the sanctity of the domestic sphere and promote heterosexual marriage.

The end of the war, the public's disillusionment with inflation, and the shadow of the atomic bomb signaled the rise of film noir with such fatalistic narratives as *Detour* (1945), *The House on 92nd Street* (1945), *Scarlet Street* (1945), *Boomerang* (1947), *The Lost Weekend* (1945), *The Snake Pit* (1948), *Out of the Past* (1947), *Dead Reckoning* (1947), *The Big Sleep* (1946), *Mildred Pierce* (1945), and *Nobody Lives Forever* (1946). As the first truly significant development in the narrative cinema since the silent era, film noir produced an explosion of counternarratives that called into question everything in social codes and heterocentric norms that cinema had constructed up to that point. In the world of film noir, no one can be trusted. Lovers betray each other as a matter of course; all business transactions are corrupt; living for whatever momentary advantage one can find is viewed as the only possible adaptation to the nuclear era. A new series of actors and types rose with the new genre, including the smoothly violent Dan Duryea, the hard-boiled Audrey Totter, the blank-faced fall guy Elisha Cook, Jr., the foredoomed Tom Neal, and the harpy Ann Savage. Indeed, film noir emerged as the most durable of the post-war genres, recreating the world of cynical manipulation that continued to be created as late as 1975 with *Farewell, My Lovely* (in which a seemingly ageless Robert Mitchum retraces the steps of Dick Powell as Philip Marlowe in 1944's *Murder, My Sweet*). Film noir recognized that the heterocentric confections of the World War II era could no longer sustain themselves in the uncertain postwar era; in their place, heterodystopian fear of the other dominated sexual and social discourse. As a postwar icon, Mitchum was as comfortable in the noirish late 1940s as he was in the post-Watergate 1970s. No matter the era, Mitchum's somnolent gaze of indifference and desire remained detached yet continuously modern. Performances of straightness in film noir were marked by violence and depravity. The world was no longer "straight," in both senses of the word. It was not until the 1990s that noir completely collapsed through the inevitable strain of unvarying repetition (only to be brought back in a series of neo-noirs, inspired for the most part by the unremittingly bleak postwar novels of Jim Thompson).

The influence of Italian neorealism led to increased location shooting. Shot for the most part outside of the studio, *All the King's Men* (1949) presented actor Broderick Crawford as a corrupt politician loosely based on Senator Huey P. Long of Louisiana. In the wake of the House Un-American Activities Committee hearings, anticommunist hysteria gripped the nation; the inflexible construct of straightness was seen as ever more crucial to maintaining the dominant social order, as demonstrated in *My Son John* (1952) and *I Married a Communist* (1949). After the war, television sitcoms introduced idealized visions of the domestic sphere into millions of American homes, with such pioneering teleseries as *I Love Lucy, I Married Joan, My Three Sons, Father Knows Best,* and numerous other home-centered comedies. This pattern prevailed through the 1960s to the present, in *Happy Days, Dharma and Greg, Laverne and Shirley, The Love Boat, Fantasy Island,* and numerous other heterosexually based sitcoms.

After the war, it was no longer necessary to leave home to see a movie. Old movies started to appear on television, and an entirely new cycle of

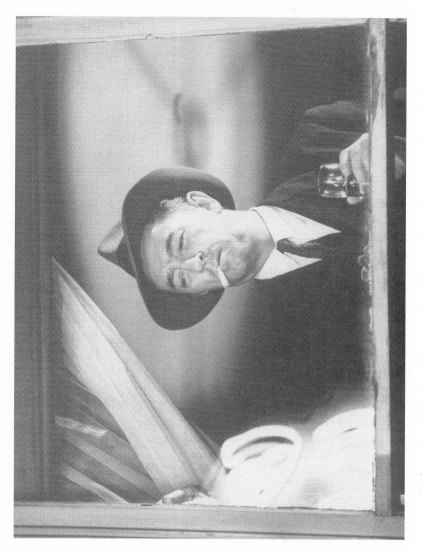

FIGURE 6. The ageless Robert Mitchum in *Farewell, My Lovely.* Courtesy: Jerry Ohlinger Archives.

reflexivity was born. Hollywood responded to the threat of television with increasing doses of violence, sex, and spectacle, beginning a cycle with such 1940s and 1950s films as *Detective Story* (1951), *The Outlaw* (1943), *High Noon* (1952), *Destination: Moon* (1950), *When Worlds Collide* (1951), *Samson and Delilah* (1949), *The Greatest Show on Earth* (1952), *The Ten Commandments* (1956), *Forbidden Planet* (1956), and other spectacularized, hypersexualized genre films. Since the advent of *Star Wars* (1977), such films have transformed the theatrical cinematic landscape into a zone of unrelenting, overamplified spectacle devoid of plot, characterization, or overriding human agency. The James Bond series, begun in 1962 with *Dr. No,* introduced viewers to a new level of violence and sexual license: the license, indeed, "to kill" and to have sex with as many consensual partners as possible. As Bond, Sean Connery created a character composed of equal parts misogyny, sadism, and sexual rapaciousness, a construct that was considerably diluted when Roger Moore took over the role. Clint Eastwood, after years of television work in the resolutely heterosexual series *Rawhide,* equaled Connery's brutality and detachment as the "man with no name" in *A Fistful of Dollars* (1964), *For a Few Dollars More* (1965), and *The Good, the Bad, and the Ugly* (1966). These created a new genre of westerns, devoid of plot and/or characterization. Eastwood's character was ever more amoral than Connery's Bond—raping, pillaging, and exacting torturous revenge without a word and without apparent motive. In *Point Blank* (1967), Lee Marvin apparently returns from the dead, a modern-day Orpheus. In his search for his share of the loot from a holdup gone wrong, he ruthlessly kills all who would impede his quest.

In the early 1990s, a new series of heterosexual stereotypes emerged in the cinema, as rigidly characterized in their own way as the archetypes of the 1920s and 1940s were in their era. Quentin Tarantino reinvented heterosexual "cool" in his nihilistic vision of contemporary social commerce, *Pulp Fiction* (1994); he then scripted Robert Rodriguez's apocalyptic vampire tale *From Dusk Till Dawn* (1996). Romance was refigured in such recent films—black comedies and dramas—as *Things to Do in Denver When You're Dead* (1995), *Beautiful Girls,* and *Flirting with Disaster* (both 1996). A new generation of heterosexual icons were born, including Gwyneth Paltrow, Jennifer Jason Leigh, Meg Ryan, George Clooney (the updated reconfiguration of Cary Grant), Christina Ricci, Kurt Russell, Bruce Willis, Lili Taylor, Marisa Tomei, Brad Pitt, Michelle

Pfeiffer, Nicolas Cage, Elisabeth Shue, Sharon Stone, Sean Penn, Leonardo DiCaprio, Tom Hanks, and numerous other performers who are nothing so much as echoes of past stars. Bruce Willis and Kurt Russell are macho action stars in the tradition of John Wayne and Gary Cooper, while Sharon Stone replicates Joan Crawford's adherence to the star system, complete with attitude and overwrought histrionics. Tom Hanks replaces James Stewart. All of these actors portray a series of stereotypical roles as carefully choreographed as those of the stars of the 1920s and 1930s, demonstrating that these heterosexual archetypes sustain remarkable generic durability.

With the sole exception of the negativism inherent in film noir, presaged to some degree by the unrelenting cynicism of the pre-Code films, the heterosexually based Hollywood construct of courtship, marriage, and (on occasion) deception remained a reliable constant. Yet with the rigidly enforced gender roles circumscribed by the dominant cinema, is not all social intercourse (sexual and otherwise) predicated on a series of lies and omissions? With the heterosexual couple centered in conventional cinema, all other voices and negotiation strategies are de-narrated, pushed to the edges of the frame—or past it—in the ostensible defense of the ideal family unit.

> In the broad terrain of "America," the tension produced through this contradiction allows for various discourses to gain visibility in U.S. culture—the inculcation of seemingly marginalized voices acting as the necessary proof of "America's" democratic possibility. . . . "America," in other words, becomes the repository for its own ideological and rhetorical ideals, the means for the reification of "nation." But it is not only so-called dominant discourses that partake in this reification, for the process of articulating "America" has been a crucial component in the construction and negotiation of counterdiscourses as well. . . . Indeed, it is the inability of "America" to function as a transhistorical sign that necessitates its reiterative production. (Wiegman 131–33)

This unceasing repetition leads inevitably to narrative and generic exhaustion, and one could easily argue that the cinema long ago passed the point of no return in this regard, preferring to hypertextualize the constant reifications of each repeated narrative construct with an excess of spectacle, both aural and visual. Films of the new millennium have quite transparently abandoned any real sense of closure in their construction, the better to allow for the creation of an endless series of sequels. In insisting on open endings in contemporary Hollywood cinema, film-makers produce only the illusion of an ending and the phantom sense of "containment" that the audience desires. Yet any closed system of values, like that created by the heterocentric mold of Hollywood, inevitably leaves contested ground. Janet Staiger points out that a "conclusion to a film or a narrational voice may produce containment. . . . However, the struggle for that containment is filled with opportunities and options for individuals of varied sexes, gender identities, and sexual preferences" (16–17). Thus, narrative closure remains illusory, and the uneasy triumph of the heterosexual couple is by no means assured. The "opportunities and options" presented but not pursued by the film's narrative structure gesture toward an entirely different "ending," in which the couple is as much at risk as are the competing discourses, however faintly articulated. In the 1950s,

> In [director] Douglas Sirk's words, "America was feeling safe and sure of herself, a society primarily sheltering its comfortable achievements and insti-tutions." Hollywood acknowledged the nature of the crisis by resorting des-perately to technical innovations and gimmicks to lure audiences away from the television and out of the home. It is perhaps no accident that the 1950s are marked by the particular resurgence of the family melodrama, the Hol-lywood genre associated with the dramas of domesticity, woman, love and sexuality. While Hollywood put a brave and colourful face on its difficulties, filling the wide screen with Western landscapes and spectacular casts of thousands, the melodrama drew its source material from unease and contra-diction within the very icon of American life, the home, and its sacred fig-ure, the mother. (Mulvey 63–64)

Thus it is that, in the same way, in an environment that is supposed to suppress difference, the US military in World War II tacitly acknowl-edged and even exploited differentiated sexual and gender constructs while simultaneously presenting to the public the image of a completely hetero-sexualized fighting machine, ready to defeat the enemy (more othering) to the death. The 1940s war films, especially *Thirty Seconds over Tokyo* (1944), *A Walk in the Sun* (1945), and *They Were Expendable* (1945), so effectively promulgated this fictional image of heterosexualized coherence that, while gays and lesbians were being assimilated into the wartime mil-itary, they were still not overtly acknowledged. So effective was the campaign of images that, thirty years after the war, Hollywood was still recy-cling these same glyphs in such films as *Midway* (1976), which intersperses "reels of stock shots from *Thirty Seconds over Tokyo,* antique Japanese war films, and actual wartime footage" into a transparently fraudulent fictive construct centering on a young ensign's love for a Japanese woman. The film features "Charlton Heston, Henry Fonda, James Coburn, Glenn Ford, Hal Holbrook, Robert Mitchum, Cliff Robertson, Toshirô Mifune, Robert Wagner, Edward Albert, Robert Webber, Ed Nelson, James Shigeta, Monte Markham, Christopher George, Glenn Corbett, Tom Sel-leck, Kevin Dobson, Pat Morita, Dabney Coleman, Erik Estrada, Steve Kanaly," and many other Hollywood stalwarts (Maltin 856).

This reperformance of war can also be linked to the ritual reperfor-mance of those acts that reaffirm the dominant model of heterosexual social conduct within marriage, which in itself is essentially a public affir-mation of one's adherence to and belief in the rites and traditions of the American family unit. Recent "reality" television shows—*Big Brother, Survivor, Fear Factor,* and *Boot Camp,* for example—also indulge in the reperformance of gestures and actions to create a more lasting impression on the public. In a public lecture on 7 May 2001, the producer of *Sur-vivor* admitted that body doubles were used for cast participants in cer-tain sequences to create overhead helicopter shots or other spectacular visuals, without the knowledge of the cast members. As media critic Brian Lambert reported,

> At a Museum of Television and Radio panel in New York . . . *Survivor* pro-ducer Mark Burnett revealed that he used stand-ins/body doubles to re-cre-ate scenes for his supernaturally-hyped [sic] TV series. . . .
>
> "I'm not embarrassed about it," Burnett told an audience gathered to discuss the mildly Kafkaesque topic of "What Is Reality on Television"? "It didn't change the outcome of the race," he said, referring to "stunt contes-tants" tossed into the water to grab a few new angles on an open water swim-ming competition.
>
> He was asked how much manipulation is allowable in "reality TV" before it becomes . . . something else.
>
> "I don't know what the line is," he replied. "I'm just making entertain-ment." (B. Lambert)

The crew "documenting" the perils endured by the first group on *Sur-vivor* even went so far as to use the actual shirts, hats, and other clothing worn by the "cast members" in their recreations, subsequently returning the garments to the show's participants for their personal use.

In the ultimate public act of compulsive heterosexuality, the Fox network has recently inaugurated a highly successful series of broadcasts entitled *Surprise Wedding*. An unsuspecting swain is led out in front of a live studio audience to meet his ostensible beloved, who is clad in a traditional white wedding gown, for an ambush marriage. As the show progresses, the men are separated from their intended brides in isolation chambers to mull over the situation, and the brides-to-be make desperate remote-video pleas to the men, literally begging them to submit to the ritual—an *actual* marriage on live network television. As the host quipped on *Surprise Wedding II,* "[S]ome marriages are made in Heaven; others are made on Fox." Implicit in this statement is the irony that these weddings may well be disasters. Yet just as we can't look way from car crashes, viewers are compelled to watch these disasterous beginnings. If the male backs out, he is considered a poor sport for not completing the ceremony; the would-be brides are led off the stage weeping (followed into the wings by a battery of video cameras that document their every gesture and emotion). In its insistence on marriage as the logical outcome of all female-male relationships, and in its slavish devotion to the iconic supremacy of a wedding in white, *Surprise Wedding* omits nearly all references to courtship or to a relationship between the two people about to be married. Its focus is solely on the ceremonial aspect of the union, complete with a solicitous minister wearing a clerical collar. Just as these weddings can be performed and reperformed in reruns without narrative context, so does Fox reperform (again and again, from various angles and at various speeds, from normal to frame-for-frame slow motion) a litany of disasters in *Maximum Exposure:* horrific car and boating accidents, explosions, and other natural and unnatural disasters, complete with sarcastic voice-over by the never-seen but omnipresent narrator. Footage of an avalanche destroying a house is presented with the commentary "Home, sweet home . . . oops, no home!"; car bombs repeatedly explode from multiple angles ("Let's see that again!"), killing several policemen again and again, all for the viewer's amusement. As with *Surprise Wedding,* no context for the events is given; it is just a fistfight or a car crash or an explosion—or a wedding. All is performance and climax; the context, the sole thread that strings performances into a semicoherent whole, is provided by the viewer's voyeuristic impulse. The events presented have been so abstracted, so removed from the actual that only the memory of their performance remains—all is a drag act, whether straight or gender bent. And yet what can truly be represented here, in the domain of the look and nothing else, other than the actions of the protagonists, devoid of any personal history or significance?

While the American cinema has a long history of ignoring and/or suppressing sexual and racial differences, the British cinema, with its numerous colonialist strategies, has also sought to uphold an inequitable system of class and race coding through the usual brace of heterocentric romances and dramas. Yet the British cinema has also allowed for the existence of ruptures within the overall system of signification, especially in the area of drag acts and queer performativity. This is evidenced in the *Carry On* films of the late 1950s (when the events of World War II were only a decade old) to the late 1970s (when "camp" was being overtaken by a more aggressive and more transgressive cinematic movement, as exemplified by the films of Derek Jarman). At the center of the *Carry On* films were two actors with polar personalities: Kenneth Williams and Sidney James. In their pairing in most of the *Carry On* films, Sid James projects a sense of overzealous straightness in all of his interactions with the other characters, while Kenneth Williams, a flamboyant, "outed" gay man in real life, plays up to his own camp persona.

Immensely popular in Britain upon their initial release, the *Carry On* films have grown into a cult series, idolized by many of the younger generation of British comics. As Williams himself wrote in his diaries, "[D]oing these *Carry On* films is as though nothing has changed since '57, when I started the first one. Since then, as a style of burlesque they've established themselves as part of the British entertainment scene and they have made a way of life possible for me" (*Diaries* 272). For readers not familiar with the *Carry On* films, a brief digression into their structure is in order. Beginning with *Carry On, Sergeant* (released in 1958), the format of the series was almost immediately established. Robert Ross summarizes the mix of characters neatly: "[Kenneth] Williams (the snobbish intellectual), [Kenneth] Connor (the bumbling boy of nerves), [and Charles] Hawtrey (the slightly effeminate beanstalk)" (R. Ross, *Carry On* 14), to which would be added in subsequent installments of the series Sidney James (the lecherous Cockney good old boy), Hattie Jacques (one of film's most memorable "stout" comediennes), Leslie Phillips (the wolfish man-about-town), and Joan Sims (the put-upon housewife). Romantic interest was supplied by Jim Dale, the perennial dashing leading man of the series, and a variety of ingénues, including Shirley Eaton and Sally Douglas. Other members of the troupe included Peter Butterworth, Angela Douglas, Barbara Windsor—especially in the films from the mid to late 1960s—and the occasional guest star (Roy Castle, Phil Silvers, Elke Sommer) to keep the mix fresh. These actors were, of course, just a few of the many who appeared in the *Carry On* films, but with these persons the formula was firmly established. All the films were directed by Gerald Thomas and produced by Peter Rogers. Shooting almost invariably took place at Pinewood Studios, with a minimum of location sequences. The budgets were always minuscule.

The basic formula was simple: throw a group of mismatched incompetents into a situation, and then use as many wheezy old gags as possible, with a great deal of blue humor. Talbot Rothwell was responsible for most of the series' scripts, which shamelessly recycled music-hall routines, old radio shows, and even material from previous films. The humor, though broad, was never vulgar. *Carry On, Sergeant,* was a military farce; *Carry On, Nurse* (1959), used copious amounts of bedpan humor; *Carry On, Teacher* (1959), found the group as misfit schoolmasters; *Carry On, Constable* (1960), had the gang pressed into police service; *Carry On, Cabby* (1963), had the troupe running rival taxi services; *Carry On Spying* (1964) was a James Bond spoof; *Carry On, Cleo* (1964), recycled not only the plot but also many of the same costumes and sets as *Cleopatra* (1963; directed by Joseph L. Mankiewicz); *Carry On, Cowboy* (1965), spoofed westerns; *Carry On Screaming!* (1966) spoofed Hammer horror films. On and on it went, year after year. Even Sidney James's near-fatal heart attack in 1967 created only a blip in the series, which effortlessly cruised through most of the 1970s repeating the original 1950s formula.

By 1971, brief bits of nudity were creeping into the series, and the scripts became even more recycled and more vulgar, losing much of the innocent double-entendre humor that had given the series its relatively innocent charm. *Carry On, England* (1976), is perhaps the series' low point, as series regular Jack Douglas noted in an interview years later. "Peter Rogers decided to broaden the style of comedy. I always thought that everything should be left to the imagination[;] . . . the other regulars [and I] were very concerned during the scene where the girls take their tops off[;] . . . they went too far and the comedy was lost" (qtd. in R. Ross,

Carry On 121). *Carry On, England,* and its failure at the box office, was followed by a compilation film of highlights from the series, *That's Carry On* (1977). This was the final film in the series to be distributed by Rank. When *That's Carry On* too flopped, it became clear to one and all that the formula's time had finally passed.

A last effort in the original series, *Carry On, Emmannuelle* (1978), was a critical and commercial failure. Critic Philip French cited it as being "put together with an almost palpable contempt for its audience. This relentless sequence of badly written, badly timed dirty jokes is surely one of the most morally and aesthetically offensive pictures to emerge from a British studio" (qtd. in R. Ross, *Carry On* 125). The film was given an AA rating by the censor, which forbid the eight-to-seventeen crowd, the series' biggest audience, access to the film; at the same time, the film was too tame for an over-eighteen crowd seeking salacious thrills (127). Kenneth Williams agreed to appear in the film only after several rewrites and a pay increase; Barbara Windsor, offered an insultingly brief appearance, declined to participate. Contemporary critics were certainly a trifle too harsh in their distaste for *Carry On, Emmannuelle;* the British "nasties" (violent "splatter" films) that would proliferate only a few years later were arguably more objectionable from a number of viewpoints. Still, it is a desperately unfunny production, substituting crass burlesque-house routines for the relatively innocent innuendo of the previous productions. It looked as if the series was over.

Fourteen years later, however, Jim Dale was enticed back before the cameras for *Carry On, Columbus* (1992), with rising comic Rik Mayall essentially standing in for Kenneth Williams. Offered only minor parts, the old series regulars declined to participate. Due to higher production values and the sentimentality of an audience hungry for a new *Carry On* film, the movie, with a £2.5 million budget, was a surprising success at the box office and brought the series to a commercially successful close. Numerous television shows and stage presentations followed the initial run of the series between 1969 and 1989. These culminated in Bernard Bresslaw and Barbara Windsor's stage appearance in *Wot a Carry On in Blackpool,* which played at the popular seaside resort from July through October 1992. In 1993, Bernard Bresslaw, Gerald Thomas, and Kenneth Connor all passed away, just as the British Film Institute acquired "production notes, original scripts, contracts, correspondence and publicity materials for the entire series" of films (R. Ross, *Carry On* 181). Several years previously, the National Film Theatre had mounted its first retrospective of the *Carry On* films, and the series also found a second life with a new generation of fans through videocassette sales.

Carry On star Kenneth Williams, while not brought up in wealth and privilege, was nevertheless a model aesthete in search of a mentor. He was born on 22 February 1926 in London, near King's Cross Station. Williams's father, Charley, managed a beauty shop, and the family lived in the modest rooms above. Originally pressed by his father to learn lithography as a trade, Williams was soon fascinated by the theater and started keeping a diary, at age fifteen, in 1942 (K. Williams, *Diaries* 1). Almost immediately, Williams waded into the waters of popular culture, observing in his very first entry that *It Started with Eve* (1941, directed by Henry Koster) was "especially good" (1). By 1943, Williams had joined an amateur theatrical troupe, the Tavistock Players (K. Williams, *Letters* 1). In February 1944, Williams was inducted into the British armed forces and spent most of World War II with the Royal Engineers as a surveyor. After the war, Williams was transferred to the Combined Services Entertainments Unit and made his stage debut as a detective in *Seven Keys to Baldpate* at the Victoria Theatre in Singapore in 1946. Williams was consciously gay from his early teens (Williams may have had his first sexual encounter in 1941, when he was billeted during the war with a retired veterinarian named Chisholm [Davies in K. Williams, *Diaries* 1]) and simultaneously fastidious in his sexual life. Williams was an intimate friend of the doomed playwright Joe Orton and worked in early productions of *Loot,* along with the usual turns in variety shows and amateur theatricals. Williams was unable to drift into casual relationships, and as his diary clearly indicates, he found his most satisfying sexual encounters in solitary masturbatory fantasies. An obsessive chronicler of his own life, Williams committed to paper his innermost thoughts, fears, and fantasies, and he clearly loathed and yet seemed a prisoner of his career. Williams's early successes included a fairly long run in *Hancock's Half Hour,* as well as numerous cabaret and music-hall revues. While radio and theatrical fame came relatively quickly, cinematic notoriety eluded Williams until he agreed to join the cast of *Carry On, Sergeant;* he followed up this film with a spirited turn as a coded gay hospital patient who eventually supervises a clandestine operation in *Carry On, Nurse.* Despite its extremely modest budget, *Carry On, Nurse,* became the highest-grossing British release of the year and then repeated this commercial success in America, a rare feat for a British production (R. Ross, *Carry On* 18). With the success of this film, coupled with his radio and television performances, Kenneth Williams's outrageously camp persona became ingrained in British popular culture, and he remained with the series for the rest of his life.

His attitude toward the *Carry On* films was always ambivalent. Paid no more than five thousand pounds for each film (except for the final disastrous entry in the series, *Carry On, Emmannuelle,* for which he received the princely sum of six thousand pounds [R. Ross, *Carry On* 128]), Williams was clearly dismissive of his work. Yet he was seemingly always willing to do another film, and then another, until they became the cinematic vehicle that defined his on-screen persona as a vain, swishy, egotistical, nasty, cowardly, supercilious twit, much the same character that Rik Mayall plays today in the *Bottom* teleseries with his partner, Adrian Edmondson.

Sidney James, in contrast, was born on 8 May 1913 in Johannesburg, South Africa, and was on the stage from the age of four. His parents were music-hall veterans, and young Sid was soon part of the act, although it was not until 1929 that he set his sights on a career in show business (R. Ross, *Complete* 11). In 1937, Sid joined the Johannesburg Repertory Players and began a long run of stage performances. By 1940, he was considered one of the stars of the company, playing the role of George in a stage adaptation of John Steinbeck's *Of Mice and Men.* On 21 March 1941, James gave his first performance in aid of the war effort in the Defense Force Entertainment Unit, becoming a member of what would soon be known as the Crazy Gang and getting his first taste of London as a member of the armed forces (R. Ross, *Complete* 12–13). Demobilized in the summer of 1945, James found himself back in Johannesburg, but the town was becoming too small for the fast-rising comic. He joined Gwen Ffrangcon-Davies's legendary theatrical troupe in 1945 and was soon given a grant of £450 to study acting in England.

Sid James landed in England on Christmas Day, 1946, and almost immediately began racking up credits in both film and theater. Astoundingly, in less than *two weeks,* James had already begun shooting his first feature film, Oswald Mitchell's *Black Memory* (1947; R. Ross, *Complete* 15, 51), in addition to accepting radio and early television assignments. Sid followed up his first feature with *Night Beat* (directed by Harold Huth, 1948), *Once a Jolly Swagman,* with Dirk Bogarde (directed by Jack Lee, 1948), Michael Powell and Emeric Pressburger's *Small Back Room*

(1948), and director John Gilling's *Man in Black* (1949). By 1951, he was sharing scenes with Alec Guinness in Charles Chrichton's classic comedy *The Lavender Hill Mob*. Gaining demand as a character actor, James chalked up a gallery of tough-talking comedy and drama performances by the late 1950s, when he accepted a part in the film *Carry On, Constable* (1960). He then found himself playing the straightest of straight men opposite the ferocious camping of Kenneth Williams, Kenneth Connor, and the delightfully fey Charles Hawtrey.

With Kenneth Williams already one of the stars of the *Carry On* films, Sid James was obliged to tailor his role in the series to fit Williams's hyperkinetic, nostril-flaring, openly gay persona, and in fact, any adjustments that James made were minor in the extreme. Both men were thoroughgoing professionals who could be relied upon to get it right on the first take, an essential ability in this tightly budgeted series. But as the films rapidly gelled into an institution (there were thirty *Carry On*s in all, plus the best-of compilation at the series' end), Williams and James became distinctly uneasy bedfellows; they respected each other but kept their distance off the set (though it can be said that both had more of an interest in show business than in anything else). The "butch" Sidney James was a perfect foil for the exaggerated camp of Kenneth Williams (my favorite pairing being James as the rough-and-ready Marc Anthony, opposite Williams as the cowardly, mincing, and obviously gay Julius Caesar in *Carry On, Cleo*—"from an original idea by William Shakespeare," acknowledges the film's credits).

Williams's over-the-top performances irritated James during filming, while Williams felt that James took himself far too seriously. Entries about James in Williams's diaries are brief and derisory. Toward the end of their joint tenure on *Hancock's Half Hour,* Hancock suddenly announced that he was firing all the regular characters on the show except for Sidney James. "[Hancock] is mad about him, and nowadys they go everywhere together," notes Williams in his diary on Monday, 10 June 1957 (132). By 23 November 1958, Williams (still engaged as an occasional guest on the program) calls the show "a general disaster. Really terrible. This team is so dreary to me now[,] . . . this crowd, esp[ecially] James & Hancock, are so listless and disinterested and their conversation is real pleb[e] stuff. I don't care for any of them at all" (146). Williams continued to do guest shots on *Hancock,* but by the summer of 1959, his role in the program had been reduced to nearly nothing—a fact that

FIGURE 7. A young Kenneth Williams pensively confronts the camera's gaze. Courtesy: Photofest.

"every man for himself" Sid James did little to correct. Noted Williams, "There is no point in my working in this set-up any more[;] . . . the atmosphere of . . . Sid James etc. is utterly stultifying to me—there is simply no point of contact—their world is totally alien to mine, and they & me [sic] are better apart" (152).

But matters changed drastically when James joined the *Carry On* cast, for *this* time Williams was the established star and James the newcomer. Williams, never one to forget a slight, cut James little slack. At the wrap party for *Carry On, Cleo*, Williams noted in his diary, "I was the only actor there—O! no—Sid James attended—but perhaps the first half of the sentence is still correct" (240). During the filming of *Carry On, Henry* (1971), Williams commented that "there is no doubt about it, on that set, I do have privileges! And I do get more fond of Gerald [Thomas] and Peter [Rogers] every time I see them. It is because, in all the years of working together, they have never lost faith in my ability" (387). Ten days later, on Friday, 13 November 1970, Williams and James had a run-in that made clear their antipathy for each other.

> While rehearsing [a scene] with [James], I ad-libbed *one line* and [James] threw his great tantrum. *"I am a serious actor!"* bit, and shouted, "Can we ever have *one* straight rehearsal?" and there was quite an atmosphere created. . . . James does this sort of thing because he is basically a very insecure man when surrounded by real actors. As he can't act himself and is fundamentally aware of his bogus nature, he really resents any kind of talent near him. (387; original emphasis)

With this sort of acrimony on the set, it is rather amazing that the two men continued to work together, but, aware that the series kept them firmly in the public eye, they soldiered on like the professionals they were.

Why—and *how*—did they work so well together despite the marked antipathy they had for one another, and why did the public so embrace them as a performing duo? The answer, I feel, lies in their essential polarity, the contrast between James's roughish lecherousness and Williams's camp outrageousness. As Julius Caesar in *Carry On, Cleo*, for example, we are introduced to Williams sitting on an improvised throne in a tent during a military campaign nursing a bad cold. As he sneezes and sniffles, he wriggles about miserably and finally declares to the audience, "Oh! I do feel *queer!*" Moments later, the stalwartly heterosexual James (as Mark Antony) enters the tent and tells Caesar that his fellow citizens are plotting the ruler's assassination. "Oh, Tony, you won't let them get me, will you?" Caesar wails. Despite Mark Antony's assurances, Williams's Caesar immediately sinks into the role of a petulant spoiled child, fearfully casting about for an adult protector. When Caesar is finally assassinated, he cries out in mock agony one of the series' most famous lines: "Infamy, infamy, they've all got it in for me!" which scenarist Talbot Rothwell actually cribbed from an old radio program.

Yet on the set, James was frustrated by what he perceived as Williams's "unprofessional behavior." As Cliff Goodwin noted of the working relationship between Williams and James, to James, "acting, even in *Carry Ons*, was something you did and went home, it wasn't something you tried to enjoy" (133). Williams's habit of making faces off-screen while James did his close-ups infuriated James, who also hated to perform drag scenes of any kind, a distinct liability for a knockabout comedian. In *Carry On—Don't Lose Your Head* (1967), a period farce set during the French Revolution, James's character was required to masquerade as a young maiden to evade the suspicions of Citizen Camembert, chief of the secret police (played by Williams). Goodwin recounts, "[A]s Sid appeared on set in a wig and dress Williams purred, 'Ooh, I couldn't half fancy you!' The camera crew joined in with wolf whistles and equally suggestive invitations. 'Shut up the lot of you,' snapped Sid. . . . 'Let's get this scene shot and out of the way.'. . . [James] felt it belittled the macho image he had taken so much trouble to develop" (133). And yet James never resorted—or apparently even thought of using—obvious antigay slurs against Williams. Difference was respected, if not directly acknowledged. As an openly gay man in 1950s and 1960s London, Williams suffered his share of insults and injuries to his pride, all the more so because he was such a public figure. Though essentially apolitical, Williams campaigned for the decriminalization of homosexuality in England and was saddened by the sight of "closeted" gays who refused to stand up and be counted (K. Williams, *Letters* 684–85). Williams would occasionally surprise James by actually praising one of his performances, particularly in the case of *Carry On, Cowboy* (1965). In this peculiar film, Williams is almost unrecognizable as the cantankerous old judge Burke (a sort of Gabby Hayes clone), while Sidney James, as the Rumpo Kid, strolls through the film with his characteristic nonchalance, cold-bloodedly killing off the peripheral members of the cast with practiced assurance. Williams felt that this was perhaps the

Carry On gang's finest hour, and James was astonished when Williams, his old antagonist, publicly hailed his work in the film.

Kenneth Williams and Sidney James defined an era in British comedy, and the archetypes they brought so vividly to life continue to be recycled in such contemporary British comedy series as *Bottom, The New Statesman,* and *The Young Ones.* There is no doubt that Williams's openly gay screen persona paved the way for a greater acceptance of homosexual rights in Britain, a cause Williams actively championed through his work for the Albany Trust (K. Williams, *Diaries* 273). At the same time, James's cheerfully decadent rakehell convinced working-class heterosexual audiences that their lives, however constricted by the bonds of the social contract and despite the drab exterior of the postwar British economy, could nevertheless contain excitement and humor. The *Carry On* films thus stand as an emblem not only for a time but also for a state of national consciousness that was crucial in shaping Britain's modern cultural identity. Behind the flimsy props and stale gags of the *Carry On* films was a world of free-spirited sexuality, a world the audiences of the time eagerly embraced. For contemporary viewers, the *Carry On* series offers a fascinating view into the social and sexual mores of 1950 to 1970 British society, just as Kenneth Williams and Sidney James both epitomize widely stratified, yet equally complementary, aspects of the human condition.

If the sound stages of Pinewood (carefully propped over and over again to achieve the effect of whatever period was deemed necessary) served as the location for the single-entendre sexual innuendo and ritualistic gender bending of the *Carry On* films, then it can be said the dusty streets of the classical Hollywood western functioned as a perennial proving ground for the trope of heterosexualized masculinity within the dominant cinema. Needless to say, the physical location of the Hollywood western does not really exist, except of course as a set. One location in particular has served as the backdrop for many of the most influential westerns made in Hollywood's most prolific period, the 1940s through the 1970s.

Just twelve miles west of downtown Tucson, Arizona, sits Old Tucson Studios, one of the oldest and most heavily utilized movie sets ever created, a location that would serve as the backdrop for a series of aggressively heterosexual narratives (the sole exception being Andy Warhol's *Lonesome Cowboys*). Originally built by Columbia Pictures in 1939 for

FIGURE 8. Sidney James as King Henry VIII in *Carry On, Henry,* with Kenneth Williams *(extreme right),* as Cromwell. Courtesy: Jerry Ohlinger Archives.

their $1.5 million production of *Arizona* (1940), starring Jean Arthur and a young William Holden, Old Tucson Studios went on to serve as the backdrop for literally hundreds of heteroperformative westerns. It became, in a sense, the cinematic incarnation of the Old West for millions of film and television viewers. Indeed, it was Columbia's desire to escape the iconic confines of Hollywood's ersatz "western towns" that led them to the outskirts of Tucson, where production designers were struck by the unspoiled beauty of the nearly limitless desert vistas. To build the *Arizona* sets, local craftspeople were hired; they worked from archival materials found in the Tucson city library. Whenever possible, authentic materials and production techniques were used to give the finished sets for *Arizona*—in reality, a whole town in miniature—the greatest degree of authenticity possible. Often, only the exteriors of the various buildings were constructed, and in some cases, just the façades of the structures served the needs of the filmmakers. The town jail, the façade of a church, and various other buildings were constructed of sun-baked adobe, and many of these original structures survive today. This was a land of constructed heterotopia, "better" and "more realistic" than the original terrain.

When production on *Arizona* wrapped in early 1940, the set laid moribund for half a decade, as the exigencies of production during World War II forced filmmakers to conserve gasoline, power, and other wartime essentials. During this period, location filming was at a minimum, and most westerns were shot on the traditional "western street" maintained by all the major (and many of the minor, such as Republic and Producer's Releasing Corporation [PRC]) studios. Oddly enough, it was *The Bells of St. Mary's* (1945) that broke the silence at Old Tucson Studios, when some location filming for this decidedly nonwestern film was accomplished at the desert studio. In the years that followed, *The Last Round Up* (1947), *Winchester '73* (1950), *Ten Wanted Men* (1955), *Apache Agent* (1956), *3:10 to Yuma* (1957), *Gunfight at the OK Corral* (1957), *Buchanan Rides Alone* (1958), *Rio Bravo* (1959), *El Dorado* (1967), and a number of other westerns were shot on location there, with each one of these films presenting a resolutely macho vision of frontier life. This renewed burst of filming activity was a direct result of the efforts of film entrepreneur Robert Shelton, working in concert with established Hollywood producer Arthur Loew. John Wayne also became a partner in the enterprise, and as a result, business at Old Tucson boomed.

As new films and television series were shot at Old Tucson, the new sets were left behind, so that in time, Old Tucson Studios became a sprawling metropolis of film production, complete with its own costume department, sound stage, and mostly full-scale railroad. Shooting at Old Tucson was efficient and easy, and producers and directors soon grew comfortable with the town's numerous streets, buildings, and scenic vistas. As Old Tucson continued to be used as the backdrop for a torrent of generic westerns, it took on a weather-beaten aspect in keeping with the strict code of heterosexual performativity that it iconically enforced. John Wayne, in particular, shot many of his late westerns here, and the sets from *Rio Bravo* still stand. The ever-expanding standing sets were also used for episodes of the television series *Little House on the Prairie, The Lone Ranger, Wagon Train, Bonanza* (in 1966, 1971, and 1972), *Death Valley Days, The High Chaparral, Gunsmoke* (in 1972–74), several episodes of the television version of *How the West Was Won* ("The Slavers," "Luke," and "Wing," 1977–79), and *Have Gun, Will Travel.* In addition to this frenetic activity, numerous nonwestern projects were shot at Old Tucson Studios, including Sidney Poitier's breathtaking film *Lilies of the Field* (1963); the bizarre horror film *Night of the Lepus* (1972; it deals with an attack of gigantic killer *rabbits* on a small midwestern town); episodes of the television series *Petrocelli* (1974–75); and even scenes for the 1976 remake of *A Star Is Born.* With all this activity, the numerous sets and locations within Old Tucson Studios, propped and represented for subsequent productions, have become ingrained on our collective cinematic consciousness as a vision of the Old West that is instantly recognizable, comfortably nostalgic, and unquestionably heterosexual.

The golden age of the western was also Old Tucson's most prolific and influential era as a motion picture production center, and such stars as Clint Eastwood, Barbara Stanwyck, Rex Allen, James Arness, and Michael Landon worked here on numerous occasions. Howard Hawks's final western, *Rio Lobo* (1970), was shot at Old Tucson Studios, although the film is far from Hawks's best work. The ultra-conservative, homophobic Wayne and Hawks did not take to rising star Jennifer O'Neill, who played the film's principal female role, and Wayne also was clearly uncomfortable working with neophyte actor Jorge Rivero as his costar. Writer and critic George Plimpton appeared in *Rio Lobo* as a bit-part heavy and documented the atmosphere of arrogance and wounded pride that the aging star and director labored under during this, their last project together

(Plimton!). Wayne was so comfortable at this point with his on-screen persona that he directed not only himself but also the other actors, showing them the "proper" way to handle shotguns, knives, and six-shooters. Yet even with the services of veteran second-unit director Yakima Canutt to assist in the film's action sequences, *Rio Lobo* exudes an air of melancholy disillusionment; it is clear that the era of the classical, resolutely heterosexual, western is over.

As the western genre began its inevitable decline into self-reflexive parody, such projects as *Three Amigos!* (1986), a comedy-western, starring Chevy Chase, Martin Short, and Steve Martin, began to dominate the production schedule. More and more, Old Tucson was being used as a location for print and television advertising shoots (for everything from the Arizona lottery to McDonald's), along with the occasional television movie (*El Diablo* [1990]), video-game shoots (Wyatt Earp's Old West [1994]), and some legitimate major studio feature projects (*Lightning Jack* [1994], *Terminal Velocity* [1994], *Timemaster* [1995], *The Quick and the Dead* [1995], and *Tombstone* [1993]). The western's popularity as a genre was waning rapidly, replaced in the public's imagination by space films and a plethora of "space westerns" including the *Star Trek* and *Star Wars* films, along with numerous other science-fiction spin-offs and imitations. Old Tucson Studios adapted to these changing times by becoming a full-fledged tourist attraction, with daily gunfight shows, a saloon with dancing girls, and an appropriately mustached sheriff, who escorted visitors on a tour of the facility and pointed out the numerous locations within the park that had been used in various productions. As with Universal City in California, the tourist business was an immediate success. By 1995, Old Tucson Studios was the single largest tourist attraction in Arizona, drawing more than a million viewers each year. More and more, the tourists were providing an important source of Old Tucson's revenue. Still, Old Tucson Studios served as a lively production center for the many television movies, advertisements, and even theatrical feature films that were still embracing the western format, until, on the afternoon of 24 April 1995, tragedy struck.

To this day, no one knows exactly how it happened, but somehow, on a sunny afternoon when the park was filled to capacity with tourists, a fire broke out in the remote back lot. It spread rapidly. Fire companies throughout Arizona responded to the blaze, but within hours, it was clear that the fire would be a major catastrophe for Old Tucson. Within

FIGURE 9. William Holden and Jean Arthur in *Arizona*, the film that established Old Tucson Studios as a location for the classic western. Courtesy: Jerry Ohlinger Archives.

twenty-four hours, nearly fifty percent of the facility was destroyed, including the sound stage, the entire wardrobe collection, and numerous buildings, sets, and props. Amazingly, no one was hurt in the blaze, but the destruction was devastating. In a single day, more than fifty years of movie history were obliterated, and one of the film industry's most complete and detailed staging areas, including all of the stores and sets on Kansas and Front Streets (two of the most popular filming locations) was almost completely destroyed. While a massive rebuilding effort was almost immediately undertaken, with impressive results, there is no question that the damage due to the fire is lasting and, in many ways, irreparable.

The fire marked the end of the classical western as a site of heterosexual performativity, for the physical backdrop of Old Tucson had become as much a part of the genre as its other iconic markers: men in black hats, sheriffs holding off the inevitable lynch mob at the town jail (a favorite scenario of Howard Hawks, in particular), and also a sense of place and identity that belonged to the western genre alone. In its violence, constant hardship, and ritualistic heterosexual rites of passage (the gunfight, the town wedding, the endless clan battles for water and grazing land), the western served as a conduct manual for the heterosexual female and male in the cinema.

What, then, is left? The industry's increasing reliance on computer-generated imagery makes the concept of standing sets and location filming outmoded, although the results lack the essential degree of verisimilitude that location filming affords any project. Visiting Old Tucson, I was struck by the contrast between the meticulous craftsmanship on the older, surviving buildings and the indifferent modern structures that had been hastily erected to replace them. As a result of the fire, Old Tucson Studios has become more than ever before, an amusement park first and a filming location second. Much of this is beyond the control of any external agency; the western as a genre is now a dicey commercial proposition, where once it was a staple of the Saturday matinee, guaranteed to bring in modest, if predictable, returns at the box office. Contemporary westerns, such as Clint Eastwood's *Unforgiven* (1992), occasionally remind us that the genre is not wholly defunct, and one could argue that a new cycle of westerns, much like Sergio Leone's cycle of spaghetti westerns of the 1960s, could easily revitalize the western in a more contemporary format. After all, Hammer Films revived Universal's moribund cycle of horror films from the 1930s and 1940s, in color and with increased doses of graphic violence, in the 1950s and 1960s. And yet with the imagistic marketplace changing so rapidly, and with films now being created entirely on digital video with green-screen computer-generated backdrops, one wonders, sadly, whether facilities like Old Tucson haven't lived out their commercial usefulness. Indeed, more and more, Old Tucson Studios seems to be a location of nostalgia, where theme park–like live presentations of actors in period dress entertain audiences of fifty and sixty year olds eager to relive the memories of their shared cinematic youth. At the same time, the low-tech, unadorned look of these live performances harkens back to the era before film, to a time when actors performed on stages lit by candle- and limelight.

As heroically heterotopic as the site of Old Tucson was, it was nevertheless the site of a truly disruptive display of homosocial performativity on at least one occasion. In 1968, Andy Warhol used Old Tucson as a setting for his gender-bending western *Lonesome Cowboys*. In fact, *Lonesome Cowboys* is still listed in the Old Tucson Studios archives as *Romeo and Juliet,* a title Warhol appropriated to keep the authorities confused during filming. Even with this precaution, Warhol received hostile, homophobic reception in Arizona. Warhol conceived of this pioneering gender-bending gay western as a takeoff on Marlene Dietrich's persona in *Destry Rides Again* (1939), with Warhol superstar Viva in the role of Ramona, a frontier woman who operates a local dancehall. She is assisted by a young "wandering cowboy" named Julian (Tom Hompertz) and her male nurse, played by underground film stalwart Taylor Mead. Ramona's antagonists are a group of young cowboys (Louis Waldon, Eric Emerson, Joe Dallesandro, Allen Midgette, and Julian Burroughs) who want to take over the town and initiate a reign of lawlessness. The sheriff (played by Francis Francine), who erratically tries to stop the outlaw rampage, plays much of the film in drag.

Warhol was able to shoot the film in Old Tucson for only one day, as it rapidly became apparent that Warhol's vision of the Old West didn't mesh comfortably with that of Howard Hawks and John Wayne. At first the Old Tucson staff tolerated Warhol's unusual production methods ("everytime they rehearse, it's a different scene" one Old Tucson prop man remarked [Bourdon 272]), but they were soon offended by the gay lifestyle of Emerson and the other members of Warhol's troupe. A local deputy sheriff was summoned to "supervise" the filming with a baleful

FIGURE 10. Eric Emerson rides through the deserted streets of Old Tucson in Andy Warhol's *Lonesome Cowboys*. Courtesy: Jerry Ohlinger Archives.

eye, while Robert Taylor, working on another part of the set for an episode of *Death Valley Days,* glowered from the sidelines. The Old Tucson staff, fearing that they would not get their horses and prop guns back, posted a guard at the gate to prevent anyone from leaving until a complete inventory was made. Despite all these difficulties, Warhol still managed to shoot thirty-five minutes of film, nearly all of which was used in the final print. The rest of the shoot was completed at Rancho Linda Vista, where police surveillance continued until the cast and crew finally completed filming and left for New York City. Released to respectable box-office returns, *Lonesome Cowboys,* the cinema's first openly gay western, is a curious footnote to the legacy of Old Tucson Studios (see Bourdon 269–77).

Old Tucson in its heyday was adaptable to nearly any filming situation: "[I]f the script calls for a family of substance, they can move right into the handsome house across the street from the marshal's office" (Lawliss 91). Indeed, "the main street of this town was designed in its entirety by Hollywood art directors. Every vista was put together with the camera in mind" (93). This level of comfort and accessibility made Old Tucson an "instant location" of unparalleled economy for western television series and television movies, which had to be shot quickly and economically to stay under budget and to meet their tightly scheduled airdates. In 1987, for example, Elizabeth Taylor and George Hamilton made a quick trip to Old Tucson Studios to film *Poker Alice,* a CBS Television movie that was shot entirely on location in the facility, using both the standing sets and the then-existing sound stage to keep the production moving along. Similar television projects, including the Marie Osmond and Bruce Boxleitner television movie *I Married Wyatt Earp* (1983), the television series *Hart to Hart,* and nonwestern projects like *Cannonball Run II* (1984) have also made use of Old Tucson's facilities. But for the most part, the studio is now more cinematic ghost town than working facility. All the members of the Old Tucson Studios staff with whom I spoke fondly remembered the high-water mark of production before the destructive blaze and simultaneously pined for another western renaissance.

The legacy of Old Tucson Studios, then, is one of a phantom zone of images, voices, and locations, reassuringly heterosexual, yet capable of being queered. Like the patriarchal figure of John Ford, the buildings of Old Tucson constantly remind us of our heterotopic imagistic heritage, even as the new century begins and the future of the western genre seems very much in doubt. While Old Tucson Studios was initially created by Columbia Pictures for a single project, it soon became a zone of heterosexual performativity for cost-conscious producers looking for an easy-to-use, premade shooting location.

CHAPTER THREE

❈

Performativity and Rupture

One of the bleakest heterosexual visions of the twentieth century belongs to the pulp novelist and screenplay writer Jim Thompson. In a memorable group of noir novels that transformed American fiction and later became the basis for neo-noir cinema, Thompson painted a grimmer-than-grim portrait of the American male under fire from every side—alcohol, the law, relationships with women. Everything conspired against Thompson. No matter where he went in his long and tumultuous life, he saw only the worst possible side of human affairs. For Thompson, life was an endurance marathon, with death the finish line.

Thompson was born on 27 September 1906 above the town jail in Anadarko, Caddo County, in the territory of Oklahoma. Thompson's father, James Sherman Thompson, was the sheriff of Caddo County, and his mother, Birdie Myers Thompson, was a schoolteacher. When Oklahoma became a state in 1907, Jim Thompson's father made a run for Congress but was defeated by his Democratic opponent. Stung by his failure, Thompson's father quit his sheriff's post and drifted south to Texas and Mexico; Thompson, along with his mother and his sister, Maxine, moved back to Burwell, Nebraska, to live with Birdie's mother and father (McCauley 19–20). Thompson idolized Birdie's father, Grandfather Myers, and constant exposure to his grandfather from early on led to a cynical outlook on life. By the time Jim Thompson was eight years old and his father had returned from an unsuccessful stint drilling for oil as a wildcatter in Mexico (20), the young boy's character had been formed. Shy and bookish, Jim Thompson hated sports, either as spectator or as participant. Thompson's father disapproved of his son's "effete" interest in books and cultural activities and constantly berated Jim for being less than a man. James Thompson's own conduct was less than exemplary, combining bravado and cowardice with a chronic unwillingness to deal with any sort of family responsibility.

When Thompson's father set up a law practice in Oklahoma City, his wife and children followed him. Soon James Sherman Thompson was back on the road searching for oil, leaving his wife and children (including Birdie's new baby, Winifred), alone to shift for themselves. The winter of 1916 to 1917 was bleak and brutal for Birdie and her brood, but surprisingly, James Sherman returned in the spring of 1917 flush with cash—he had finally struck oil (McCauley 21). Due to his trusting and somewhat naïve nature, however, the family's income remained precarious until he was hired by a local millionaire, Jake Hamon, to audit his accounts (22). Hamon finally knocked some business sense into James Sherman, and at last the family's finances came under control. By 1919, James Sherman Thompson was, against all odds, a millionaire, and he was back in politics. He moved his family to Fort Worth, Texas, and mixed in the social circle shared by Warren G. Harding.

Yet by now a complete rift had developed between Jim Thompson and his father, exacerbated by years of absence and neglect. James Sherman Thompson's performative heterosexual model of midwestern stoicism remained alien to Jim Thompson, who was increasingly drawn to writing as a trade. But this was not to his father's liking. James Thompson criticized his son's every action, finding fault with his clothing, his manners, his posture, his hobbies, and most important, his aspirations as a writer. Jim, however, kept at it. At the age of fifteen, Thompson became a published author when he sold a piece of fiction to *Judge,* a popular humor magazine of the era (McCauley 23). Shortly thereafter, in 1922, he went to work as a copyboy for the *Fort Worth Press.* He later moved to the oil and mining trade journal *Western World* (22). In the meantime, James Thompson's wanderlust had led him out onto the road again, while Birdie and her children once again remained home alone (22).

This time, however, James Thompson's luck seemed to have deserted him. Bad investments and dry oil wells quickly ate up his new fortune, and Jim was forced to seek gainful employment to help support the family. Jim's early jobs included being an errand boy at a local burlesque house and, later, a bellboy on the night shift at the Texas Hotel (McCauley 24). Jim's take-home pay was soon helping to pay the family's bills, but his father deeply disapproved of Jim's lifestyle. Being a writer was bad enough, but now Jim was running with hoodlums and bootleggers, in defiance of his father's authority and personal code of conduct. Jim began to drink heavily, favoring hard liquor, and smoked up to sixty cigarettes a day, habits he kept for the rest of his life. Jim also became popular with guests at the Texas Hotel for his ability to locate bootleg liquor and/or prostitutes at a moment's notice. Working all night at the hotel and attending high school all day gave Jim only a few hours a night to sleep. While Jim's father professed disgust at what his son had become—a pimp and a bootlegger—James Sherman Thompson knew that his protests were hollow and unrealistic. Jim's income alone was keeping the family afloat.

Despite his unusual extracurricular activities, Jim graduated from Polytechnic High School in Fort Worth in June 1925 (McCauley 26). Less than an hour after the ceremony, however, Jim collapsed at home from a combination of tuberculosis, nervous exhaustion, and advanced delirium tremens. As Jim recovered, he became even more withdrawn and bitter. Only eighteen, Jim had already seen too much of life and noted, "I hoped for the best, but expected the worst" (qtd. in McCauley 26). Following in his father's footsteps, Jim left the family and set out for a three-year stint in the West Texas oil fields, ostensibly to build up his body and improve his health. Surprisingly enough, his plan worked. When Jim returned to Fort Worth in 1928, he had gained weight and muscle and stood six feet four inches at 240 pounds (30). Yet the work had been brutal. Jim Thompson had been involved in several accidents while working in the fields but had escaped serious injury; others he worked with were not as lucky. Jim saw violent death, despair, and poverty in the oil fields—the poor being worked to death by the rich to bring in more oil, more wealth. Typically, Thompson sided with his coworkers rather than with his bosses, and by the time he departed, he had developed a lifelong hatred and suspicion of the machinations of big business (31). Because Jim had been writing all the time he had been working on the oil pipeline, he returned with some short stories that were published in *Texas Monthly* in 1929. The February 1929 issue contained Thompson's "Oil Field Vignettes," and June 1929 saw the publication of "Thieves of the Field" (McCauley 32). These were rough, early pieces, but they showed talent and promise, and Thompson was at last achieving his dream of being a published author. But fate soon dealt Jim Thompson another unexpected blow.

Thompson had returned to his old bootlegging bellboy job at the Texas Hotel, when the editor of the *Texas Monthly* advised him to drop the job and attend college instead. Maxine, Jim's elder sister, was already enrolled at the University of Nebraska, Lincoln (UNL), and had married Russell Boomer, whose father taught in the university's Agricultural College (McCauley 33). The timing proved sadly propitious. Jim's bootlegging operations at the hotel finally blew up in his face, and he was forced by prohibition agents, the hotel's management, *and* local bootleggers to leave town in a hurry. Jim skipped town with his mother and his younger sister, Winifred ("Freddie" for short). Jim's father eventually left Fort Worth on his own to drift through a variety of menial jobs.

Running from the law and his former criminal associates, Jim eventually arrived with Birdie and Freddie in Lincoln. His mother and sister returned to Burwell to live with Birdie's family, while Jim enrolled at UNL in September 1929 (McCauley 36). He majored in animal husbandry and agriculture and pledged the Alpha Gamma Rho fraternity (36). Moving into a shabby apartment above a drugstore with Maxine and Russell, Jim worked his way through school as a dime-a-dance dancer, a theater projectionist, a collection agent, a night guard at a funeral parlor, a radio salesman, a temp stenographer, a part-time writer for the *Lincoln Star,* and a baker's helper (McCauley 36; Polito 159). But UNL proved an important turning point for the young writer. Jim took, in addition to his agriculture classes, English composition with Russell True Prescott. Prescott, also an associate editor of the *Prairie Schooner,* soon took a liking to the young, highly motivated writer. Prescott hired Jim as a teaching assistant and grader, and introduced him to the members of the *Prairie Schooner* staff. At that time the *Schooner* published both student and professional works, and Thompson saw an opening. Prescott introduced Thompson to Willa Cather's work, and it was in Prescott's classes that Thompson sharpened his writing skills with the short pieces "Oswald the Duck" (fall 1929) and "The Picture" (spring 1930; Polito 151). These early efforts were promising enough that Prescott finally introduced Thompson to Lowry C. Wimberly, the founding editor of the *Prairie Schooner* (153). Thompson soon became one of "Wimberly's boys," a group of young men and women who formed an informal literary salon at Wimberly's home on R Street every other Sunday evening (153). Other members of the group included Kenneth Keller, Ben Botkin, Loren Eiseley, and William Thompson; Weldon Kees would join the group some years later (153).

Even in this select company, Thompson stood out. His rakehell personality and his fund of personal anecdotes made him one of Wimberly's most popular acolytes, and in return, Wimberly introduced Thompson to more of Cather's work, as well as to the writings of Glenway Wescott, Dorothy Canfield Fisher, William Faulkner. He also introduced him to the pulp writers whose work appeared in such magazines as *True Detective* (Polito 154), although Wimberly considered the works in *True Detective* guilty pleasures and favored less-sensational fiction. The writers in *True Detective* interested Thompson, mostly because they told of life as a series of jolts and disruptions, of hard times and hard-boiled cynicism. The heterosexualized code of heroic male behavior served as a template for all of the stories in *True Detective, Black Mask,* and the other tough-guy crime magazines. Thompson had found his model. Working feverishly, Thompson ultimately placed two stories and one poem in the *Schooner.* His poem "A Road and a Memory" appeared in the winter 1930 issue; his short story "Character at Iraan" in the spring 1930 number (McCauley 37). The poem is a somewhat awkward and sentimental reminiscence, but the story is pure Thompson—a tale from his time in the oil fields of West Texas. The narrator, a young man named Slim, becomes an alcoholic while working on the pipeline. One night, without meaning to, Slim almost kills himself by drinking too much bootleg liquor. In a near coma, he hears himself pronounced dead by his friends. The stark pessimism of "Character at Iraan" marked Thompson as an extremely raw writer, even for the early 1930s—when crime fiction and movies were becoming even more violent and brutal (until the Hays-Breen Motion Picture Production Code cracked down on both Mae West and the numerous movie gangsters of the period with the sweeping reforms of 1934).

In the fall of 1931, Thompson published his final piece for the *Schooner,* "Gentlemen of the Jungle." This short series of satirical vignettes covered "life on the rails" for a group of hoboes. It was also during this period that Thompson fell under the increasing influence of Robert Crawford, a rather eccentric figure who taught "agricultural journalism" and had helped Thompson enter the university; Crawford later lent Jim money to pay for books and tuition (Polito 150). Crawford had published an instructional volume, *The Magazine Article,* in 1931. In an essay in this volume entitled "Fiction Writing," Crawford not only offered commonsense advice about editors and markets, but also a series of precepts for what he dubbed "The Confession Article," in which the writer must put her- or himself in the protagonist's position. Wrote Crawford, "[T]o a large extent you must put yourself in the position of the person who has had the experience" being documented (qtd. in Polito 157). Thompson immediately took this advice to heart. His most important stories and novels are all tortured first-person narratives, in which Thompson climbs inside his character's consciousness and relates often-nightmarish events with both clarity and harrowing conviction.

Thompson was thus torn between the highly aestheticized writing favored by Wimberly and Prescott and the frankly commercial work to which Crawford aspired (Polito 158). Thompson knew instinctively where his own writing was going by now; he would follow the *Black Mask* writers, creating tales of hard-boiled masculine exploits in which heterosexuality was seen as normative behavior to be contrasted with the "deviance" of gay and/or lesbian subcharacters, necessary devices for moving the narrative forward. Crawford's approach became Thompson's model. Crawford taught writing as a business, while Wimberly and Prescott taught writing as an art. Given his grim and unsparing upbringing, Thompson knew that, above all, he had to write for money, and Crawford was the one who opened Thompson's eyes to the potential profits of fiction writing.

By this time, Jim had fallen in love with Lucille Boomer, Maxine's sister-in-law and George Boomer's daughter. Lucille and Jim had corresponded since Maxine's move to Lincoln in 1927, and when Jim first arrived at the university, one of his first acts was to look up Lucille and continue their long-distance conversation in person (McCauley 33). Lucille recalled in an interview with writer Michael J. McCauley, "I think perhaps I fell a little bit in love with him immediately" (qtd. in McCauley 36). Their relationship rapidly progressed from there, aided by George Boomer's liking for Jim and his work. Maxine remembered, "[M]y father-in-law at the time, Professor Boomer, thought Jimmie was a second Walt Whitman—admired him, liked him, just crazy about him" (qtd. in McCauley 39). George Boomer's enthusiasm for Jim, however, was not shared by his wife, Grace. Matters were further complicated when George

Boomer, who was not a well man, died in March 1930 (Polito 160). Jim and Lucille attended George Boomer's funeral standing side by side, but almost immediately, Grace Boomer set in motion her plans to separate the couple. As Maxine recalled, Grace Boomer "wanted her daughter to have someone with a lot of money . . . [and she] never thought Jimmie would amount to anything" (qtd. in Polito 160). Lucille admitted that "there was a period of time when it was very serious. But it wouldn't have worked out. I liked him, and I admired many qualities of his, but others not so much. . . . Jim seemed too much a vague introvert, unsettled, not really knowing where he was headed. 'Loner' describes him very well" (qtd. in Polito 160). By the fall of 1930, Lucille told Jim they were through as a couple. On Valentine's Day, 1931, she married a dental student named Walter Larson. In 1932, Lucille and Walter left Lincoln for Hartford, Connecticut. She never saw Jim Thompson again (Polito 161; McCauley 39–40).

Jim's grief was partially alleviated by the fortuitous arrival of Birdie and Freddie, who moved to Lincoln in 1930 just as Jim's relationship with Lucille was falling apart. Jim moved in with his mother and sister in a rented house at 2985 Holdrege Street (Polito 162), and Birdie began taking evening classes at the university. Jim was nevertheless inconsolable, and his interest in writing and classes waned. As his relationship with Lucille collapsed, his brother-in-law, Russell, was busy fixing up Thompson with a series of blind dates. Much to everyone's surprise, one of them turned out to be perhaps the most important meeting of Jim's life. Shortly after Lucille's wedding, when Jim was still in a melancholy stupor, he agreed to go on a blind date with Alberta Hesse, a friend of Russell's. Their first date in late February 1931 was, in Alberta's eyes at least, a great success. Jim, however, was so upset by Lucille's "betrayal" that he didn't call Alberta again until "some time in early March. . . . From that point on, you couldn't tear us apart," Alberta remembered (qtd. in Polito 163). Immediately smitten, Alberta called Jim "a handsome brute[;] . . . when I first saw him, I knew I was going to marry him" (qtd. in Polito 166), and on 16 September 1931, she did just that. Surreptitiously driving to Marysville, Kansas, the couple was married by a local justice of the peace. Alberta paid the fee for the license (twenty dollars); Jim was, as usual, low on funds. The couple celebrated with ice cream sundaes and then drove back to Lincoln for a college fashion show and an evening at the movies—Josef von Sternberg's 1931 film version of Theodore Dreiser's book *An American Tragedy*, surely an odd, yet somehow appropriate choice for the newlyweds (Polito 167).

Jim and Alberta eloped for a variety of reasons, but their main objective was to overcome the objections of *both* their families. Alberta's mother, Elena Hesse, was furious with her daughter for marrying a ne'er-do-well without prospects; Jim's sisters Freddie and Maxine were even more vociferous in their objections to the marriage, feeling that Alberta was an intellectual lightweight (Polito 167). On 6 April 1932, the couple renewed their vows in the Sacred Heart Catholic Church in Lincoln. Alberta's relatives attended the ceremony. Jim's were conspicuously absent, but with good reason: Birdie, Maxine, and Freddie had moved back to Fort Worth to take care of Jim's father, who was recovering from a broken leg, and none of them returned to Lincoln for the service. Jim and Alberta Thompson were on their own (Polito 169).

Regardless of their families' feelings, Jim was ecstatic. In 1931 alone, he wrote seven new pieces for the *Cornhusker Countryman,* the magazine of the Agricultural College of UNL (Polito 169). Jim was still only a sophomore, but he had already lived a more complex life than many people ever do, and these relaxed stories show Thompson again mining his colorful past in the oil fields and hobo jungles of Texas. It was also during this period that Thompson wrote the short story "Sympathy," which remained unpublished until the literary magazine *Bomb* finally printed it in 2000, almost seventy years after Thompson crafted it. Drawing on his experiences as a collections agent for the Kay-Bee Clothing Company, Thompson created this brutal "short short" about the efforts of agents of the Planet Credit Stores to collect on a credit purchase. In the story, Oscar Bordes is an unemployed father who purchased a nightgown on credit. His children have died in a fire *caused* by the nightgown, which had burst into flame and killed them instantly. Bordes commits suicide in response to a "sympathy" letter sent by Planet Credit's agents, a letter in which the agents simultaneously express grief at the loss of Bordes's children and still demand payment for the nightgown. The denouement of the story is nihilistic, typical of Thompson's work. Bordes wills his body to the medical college of the state university to repay the loan. Both the *Countryman* and the *Schooner* turned the story down flat as being too grisly and uncompromising, but Thompson later used similar themes in his 1954 novel, *A Hell of a Woman* (see Polito 173).

Just as Jim seemed to be getting his bearings at last, the rug was pulled out from under him again. The Kay-Bee Clothing Company declared bankruptcy, and Thompson, who was registering for his junior year with money borrowed from Robert Crawford, was unable to pay his bills. Prescott's classes decreased in size, and he was forced to fire Thompson as a grader. With job prospects drying up and a family to support (Alberta was already pregnant), Thompson was forced to drop out of UNL on 1 October 1931. He never returned to the university, and he never completed his college degree (Polito 175–76). Alberta was forced to move in with her parents, while Jim moved to Big Springs, Nebraska. There he and his father (whom he had induced to come to Nebraska to help him) tried to make a go of it running the Big Springs Theater, a local movie house. The effort was a desperate failure that plunged both father and son deeper into debt (177). On 9 September 1932, Jim Thompson's daughter, Patricia, was born, and Jim traveled back to Lincoln to be with Alberta. Jim was unable to find any work in Lincoln, and the largesse of Professors Crawford and Prescott was at an end. He again left Alberta and his daughter at her parents' house, seeing only one way out—like his father, he had to hit the road to look for work. And so, in late September 1932, Jim left Lincoln as a hobo on a freight train. He would never return.

When Jim and Alberta were finally reunited, it would be in a rented apartment in Oklahoma City in 1933. During the intervening time, Thompson had been riding the rails and writing numerous articles for the trade journals *Nebraska Farmer* and *Oklahoma Farmer-Stockman* (Polito 183–85). By dint of sheer hard work and persistence, Thompson had finally managed to eke out the most meager of existences, but at least he was working at the trade of his choice: writing. Most important perhaps, he had also completed the first draft of a pulp thriller, "The Unholy Grail," which much later he would redraft and redraft into his novel *Nothing More Than Murder* (Polito 185).

Firmly launched on his career, Thompson later remembered his time in Lincoln and Burwell with a mixture of nostalgia and cynicism. In 1942, after working as director of the Federal Writer's Project in Oklahoma and then throwing that job over to try his luck in New York, Thompson wrote *Now and on Earth*, his first novel. In it, he noted, "Hell, in case you're interested, is actually the College of Agriculture of the University of Nebraska. You can take my word for it" (qtd. in Wolgamott 15). In the early 1950s, Thompson entered his most prolific and successful period as a writer working for Lion Books, whose editor in chief, Arnold Hano, recognized in Thompson a talent that needed only the surety of a reliable outlet. Between 1952 and 1955, Thompson published thirteen novels, including the classic hard-boiled thrillers *The Killer Inside Me* (1952), *A Hell of a Woman* (1954), *Savage Night* (1953), *After Dark, My Sweet* (1955), *The Golden Gizmo* (1954), *A Swell Looking Babe* (1954), *Recoil* (1953), *The Kill-Off* (1957), and my favorite, *The Alcoholics* (1953). In *The Alcoholics,* in typically sardonic Thompson fashion, a man seeking a cure for his alcoholism enters a sanitarium run by an alcoholic, who seeks only to drain his "patients" of their cash; he keeps them drunk, and then kicks them out on the street when their funds are exhausted. All of these brilliant, disturbing, obsessive novels are drenched in hypermasculine performativity in which a man's life is under constant assault from societal regulations and conflict is inevitable. If heteronormative behavior was Thompson's starting point in his works, it existed only to be undermined by murder, alcoholism, incest, drug addiction, psychotic delusions, paranoia, lust, and a host of other human failings that Thompson used to create his vision of the world as a living hell. Safety is transient; loyalty is meaningless; duty and honor lead only to ruin. Thompson's best work mines the darkest recesses of the human condition and rises above the level of ordinary detective pulp fiction. Murder there is, and violence and sex and corruption, but Thompson's true territory is the human mind and how it snaps under pressure.

Thompson also wrote (or cowrote; there is much dissension on this point) two early films for director Stanley Kubrick, *The Killing* (1956) and *Paths of Glory* (1957), in addition to writing scripts for the teleseries *Dr. Kildare* and *Mackenzie's Raiders.* Later novels, especially *The Grifters* (1963) and *The Getaway* (1958), have been made into superb films (although Thompson, still alive when Sam Peckinpah directed *The Getaway* in 1972, profited little from the project; his proposed screenplay for the film was rejected by the studio, which had someone else redraft it). Of all the films made of Thompson's work, perhaps Stephen Frears's version of *The Grifters* (1990) and Maggie Greenwald's adaptation of *The Kill-Off* (1989) are the best. Frears's film is a big-budget classical Hollywood film but without any sort of a happy ending. Working from a fairly faithful screenplay by crime novelist Donald E. Westlake, Frears creates a hellish vision of a two-bit conwoman, Lilly Dillon (Anjelica Huston), and her estranged son, Roy (John Cusack). The two are constantly on the prowl

FIGURE 11. John Cusack and Anjelica Huston as mother-and-son con artists in Stephen Frears's film *The Grifters*, based on the novel by Jim Thompson. Courtesy: Jerry Ohlinger Archives.

for new scams as they struggle to survive; their small-time cons barely keep them afloat. Lilly's existence is dominated by her menacing boss, Bobo Justus (Pat Hingle), who threatens Lilly with death when she skims off part of his take on a racetrack scam. When Lilly repeats her mistake, Bobo sends his hit men to dispose of her and she flees. Desperate for cash, she plays on her son's Oedipal fixation; she tries to seduce him to get his help in making a new start in another town. But Roy resists, and while pretending to offer a farewell toast, Lilly makes a last desperate attempt to steal Roy's cash. She accidentally severs Roy's jugular vein with a chipped glass. Momentarily stricken by remorse, Lilly recovers almost immediately, scoops up Roy's bankroll, steals a car, and disappears into the night. Lilly's life will be one of continual flight; another town, another Bobo. Lilly cannot afford the luxury of maternal concern, not when her own life is at stake.

In *The Kill-Off,* the life of a small town is stage managed by the morbidly obese Luane (Loretta Gross). Barking orders and spreading lies and rumors through her telephone, she controls the destinies of the film's characters from her enormous, filthy bed. *The Grifters* is slick and polished but remains resolutely downbeat; at the film's end, the mother has killed her son, stolen his money, and skipped town to drift in anonymity for the rest of her drab existence. *The Kill-Off,* by comparison, is as cheap as a Lion twenty-five-cent original paperback, with a cast of unknowns and threadbare production values, redeemed solely by the strength of the performances in the film and by Greenwald's uncompromising embrace of Thompson's vision. Nevertheless, *The Kill-Off* is faithful to Thompson's incisive and unrelenting critique of the heterosexual white nuclear family.

In his own lifetime, Thompson never saw anything like these two films in terms of fidelity to his brutal originals. Thompson felt to the end of his days that Kubrick had cheated him out of credit for the screenplay of *The Killing* (see Polito 398–99), giving him only an "additional dialogue" credit for what Thompson and others perceived as a solid collaboration. Although Thompson received full credit for his work on Kubrick's *Paths of Glory* (400), "screenplay by Stanley Kubrick and Jim Thompson," he never really forgave the reclusive auteur for what he perceived as a "betrayal" of their working relationship. But if one wonders why Thompson continued to work with Kubrick after *The Killing,* the answer, as always, is very simple. He needed the work.

In his last years, Jim Thompson kept writing at a furious pace. He also appeared as an actor in *Farewell, My Lovely* (1975, directed by Dick Richards), the third screen adaptation of Raymond Chandler's novel of the same name. Thompson portrayed Judge Baxter Wilson Grayle, the cuckolded but politically powerful husband of the much younger Helen Grayle (Charlotte Rampling). Thompson's ex-agent, Jerry Bick, arranged this brief role as a favor, so that Thompson would be eligible for medical care through the Screen Actors Guild. Thompson also kept a file of projected novels in his desk, with thirty pages written for each new work; when presented with a contract, Thompson would finish the project. He wrote novelizations (including one for the teleseries *Ironside*) and other potboilers to keep the bill collectors at bay, but finally, worn down by illness and alcohol, Jim Thompson died on 7 April 1977 in Los Angeles.

Jim Thompson's vision of heterosexuality as a sort of existential hell is uniquely nihilistic, but it finds a complementary voice in the films of Robert Downey, Sr., who has been working on the margins of the mainstream cinema for the past forty years. Perhaps America's most uncompromising satirist since Preston Sturges, Robert Downey, Sr., created in the early 1960s and 1970s a series of brutally funny, no-holds-barred satires that examined the roles of sex, race, and performativity in modern American culture. Downey was born in New York City on 24 June 1936 to a mother who was a Powers model and a father who was a restaurant manager. When he was in his teens, Downey's sole interests were baseball and boxing, and he dropped out of high school when he "ran into geometry or something." "I just knew that it was something I wasn't interested in . . . [and] I was happy to get out. So I joined the army" (Downey). But life in the relentlessly straight army wasn't easy for the filmmaker.

By his own admission, Downey "served a lot of time in the stockade for being a drunk," but these periods of incarceration actually served as his first introduction to the possibilities of being a creative artist. One of the guards in the lockup gave Downey a notebook and a pen and suggested he pass the time by writing some essays. Instead, Downey began work on a series of one-act plays. After a bad-conduct discharge and one summer as a pitcher in semipro baseball in Pittsburgh, Pennsylvania, Downey headed back to New York, where one of his early plays—*What Else Is There?*—was produced off-off Broadway. The play was, according to Downey, "kinda wild, pretty ahead of its time[;] . . . the actors played missiles, in silos, ready to go off." During the production, Downey met early collaborator William Waering, who suggested that the two men make a movie using Downey's script and Waering's 16mm camera. Downey proceeded to make a series of films that anarchically disrupt and critique "norms" of American culture, including race, sexuality, authority, and film narrative itself.

Their first film, *Balls Bluff* (1961), was a thirty-minute silent in which a Union Civil War soldier finds himself transported to twentieth-century New York. When the lead actor failed to show up for shooting, Downey took over the role of the soldier. The film was eventually screened at various underground theaters in Manhattan. Emboldened by the success of his first project, Downey grabbed veteran underground comic Taylor Mead and drove to Washington, DC, in the fall of 1963. There they shot *Babo 73* (released in 1964), Downey's first sound feature, about a newly elected "President of the United Status [sic]." Once again, William Waering was his coconspirator. Taylor Mead, who also appeared in such legendary films as Ron Rice's *Flower Thief* (1960) and Andy Warhol's *Lonesome Cowboys* (1968), took to the role with his usual flamboyant abandon. Without press passes or permits, Downey and Waering photographed Mead wandering in and around the White House. "Kennedy was in Europe, so nobody was too tight with the security. We ran around shooting whatever we could with impunity, and even threw Taylor in with some real US generals, who didn't like what Taylor was doing at all, and they eventually kicked us out" (Downey). As he did in Warhol's films, Taylor Mead improvised much of his dialogue on the spot, and his openly gay persona predictably clashed with the straight generals, as Downey had expected. The hour-long film cost a mere three thousand dollars to make.

Critical response was enthusiastic. Brendan Gill in the *New Yorker,* raved,

> Mr. Downey clearly prefers a lot of near misses to a few direct hits, and in the course of his wild tale about the tribulations of a newly elected President of the United Status [sic] he takes bold swipes at, among other targets, the Catholic Church, the civil-rights movement, international diplomacy, *Time,* God, shoe-fetishism, psychiatry, the South, the North, the East, and the West. I laughed all around the compass . . . the funniest movie I've seen in months[;] . . . Taylor Mead looks like a cross between a zombie and a kewpie and speaks as if his mind and mouth were full of marshmallow. (qtd. in New American Cinema Group 45–46)

Despite the glowing reviews, the film didn't make any money. To make ends meet, Downey matter-of-factly accepted a commission to direct a 16mm soft-porn feature entitled *The Sweet Smell of Sex* (1965) for producer Barnard L. Sackett. The title was an obvious play on *The Sweet Smell of Success* (1957), and Downey seized upon the assignment to make a satire of the entire porn industry, much to the producer's displeasure. Sackett wanted a straight, soft-core porn film (hard-core porn was still illegal), but Downey refused to be co-opted by the producer's demands. He instead produced a film that criticized performative heterosexuality and the porn industry itself, as the film's publicity materials made manifestly clear. The blurbs promised a

> drama of people who claw their way to the bottom. Bebe Katsafannis is a bumptuous [sic] girl, with normal tastes, who comes to New York for Flag Day. Her troubles begin when she stays with her old girlfriend from Indiana, headline stripper, "Smokey La Bare.". . . A regular guy—Joe—has been following Bebe hoping that she'll straighten out and give him a break. But he is too much of a regular guy for Bebe. . . . [Eventually,] Bebe gets tired of the Big City; Joe catches her as she is about to board the bus home. . . . [T]he ordinary Joe, so *straight,* will leave the most lasting impression on her. (Sackett qtd. in New American Cinema Group 130–31; my emphasis)

Even in the bizarre world that Downey created for *The Sweet Smell of Sex,* "straight" Joe is seen as preferable to the gallery of manipulative psychotics Bebe is forced to confront. But Downey's real motivation for making the film was more basic. "I actually did *Sweet Smell of Sex* to pay for the birth of my son [actor Robert Downey, Jr.], because when my daughter was born it was tough; it was in Bellevue, and because of the film, I was able to put his mother [Elsie Downey] in a decent hospital, and that's what that was really about" (Downey). The film played Forty-second Street grind-house theaters in a 35mm blow-up format, but Downey was understandably indifferent to the film's fate.

Bouncing back from this detour, Downey made his breakthrough feature, *Chafed Elbows,* in 1966. The plot, according to Downey's brief synopsis, deals with a "man who marries his mother; they go on welfare, and it all breaks into a musical." The film stars George Morgan as Walter Dinsmore, a hapless sad sack whose sole dream is to live on welfare; in a typically bizarre casting decision, Downey's wife Elsie plays all the female roles. The opening scene of the film accurately encapsulates the entire work. Downey shows us an apparently married couple sleeping in a double bed, when the alarm clock goes off. Wearily, Walter Dinsmore drags himself out of bed, puts on some clothes, and prepares to go to work. Just as he is about to leave the room, he turns back to address the woman, who is still dozing in bed. "Good-bye, Mother," Walter deadpans, as direct and emotionless an acknowledgment of incest as the cinema has ever afforded the viewer. Nothing is treated for shock value but rather is presented in a matter-of-fact, nonjudgmental fashion. Indeed, the viewer comes not only to sympathize with Walter and his mother but even to envy them, as they drift through life oblivious to conventional heterosexual rules and regulations and concocting their own warped heterotopic paradise. Produced for less than twenty-five thousand dollars, the film was composed mostly of stills shot on a 35mm Oxberry printer, with live-action 16mm footage interspersed to keep the narrative moving. The film was an even bigger hit than *Babo 73* and ran for months at Manhattan's Gate Theatre. Rhapsodized Jules Feiffer, "[O]n the basis of *Chafed Elbows,* the one film of his that I've seen, there's good reason to believe that Bob Downey [is] the funniest filmmaker in America." Other reviews were equally enthusiastic: Archer Winsten in the *New York Post* called the film "freewheeling, hard swinging and wild," while even the staid Bosley Crowther praised the film's "lively acid wit" in the *New York Times* (qtd. in New American Cinema Group 46).

Putney Swope (1969), the director's first 35mm film, was shot mostly at night in various office buildings in Manhattan on a budget of a quarter of a million dollars. The plot revolves around Putney Swope (Arnold Johnson), a minor functionary at a huge ad agency, who is accidentally voted in as chairman of the board when the founder dies. No one on the board can vote for himself, and they don't want to vote for each other, so they all vote for Swope, the agency's token African American, on the assumption that no one else will vote for him. Seizing the reins, Swope fires everyone except for the exquisitely corrupt lifer, Nathan (Stan Gottlieb), and fills all the vacant slots with African Americans. Swope renames the shop the Truth and Soul agency (or, as he puts it, "TS, Baby!"), and wins his first new client, electronics magnate Wing Soney, with a successful pitch for Soney's new "'Get Outta Here' mousetrap." The idea is actually Nathan's, but when Soney "digs it," Swope instantly claims credit for the concept and fires Nathan. Swope repeats this pattern of idea theft continually throughout the film. By the end of the film, Swope is completely selling out, pushing war toys and the Borman Six (a huge gas-guzzling car), and even marrying a woman he doesn't like (Laura Greene) just to get ideas from her for ads. Downey's premise in *Putney Swope* is simple—everyone is equally rotten and on the take—and the film remains one of the most effective satires on heterosexual advertising ever produced.

In the opening scene of the film, a consultant hired by the firm, dressed in full S and M leather gear, delivers a lecture on why American men like to drink beer. "It's dicky pee-pee," he says flatly, and walks out the door with a huge check. All of Truth and Soul's ads are designed to appeal to the lowest-common-denominator viewer; they present sex, violence, and vulgarity in an unending succession of overtly manipulative commercials. Everyone is trying to hang on to their jobs in an environment that no one really controls. By the film's end, even Putney Swope is disgusted by his own corruption and he abruptly abandons the agency (though he leaves with a duffel bag packed with money). Short, brutal, and uncompromising, the film was original and remains effective today. For Downey, the corrupting force of social power is inherently linked to notions of heteroperformativity.

But Downey had a problem shooting *Putney Swope:* his lead actor could not remember his lines. Anyone else would have panicked, but Downey pressed on after a conference with his cameraman.

> Arnold [Johnson] never learned his lines. He couldn't. He just didn't; he couldn't, so the cameraman [Gerald Cotts] one night said to me—he knew I was upset—I said, "Jesus, I can't make any fucking sense out of this," and he said, "Well, look through here," and I looked through the viewfinder. He said, "You see that beard moving?" I said, "Yeah," and he said "You can put *anything* in there. Including what you *wrote*. But you gotta do it later. Don't waste your energy now getting upset." So I would come in every night—we shot most of the film at night—and [Arnold] would say, "I've got the lines." And I would say, "Oh, good," and then I knew he didn't. He would get pieces of it. But we just kept shooting after that, and then I dubbed the whole thing in later. But it was my voice all the way through. (Downey)

In *Putney Swope,* Downey also refined a practice that I call *repetition humor,* taking certain gags and using them over and over again, essentially running them into the ground until they stop being funny.

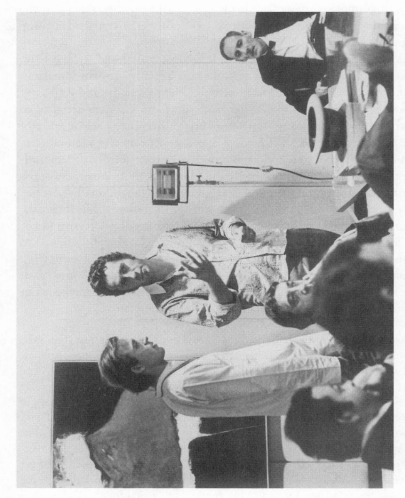

FIGURE 12. Robert Downey, Sr. *(center)*, gesturing on the set of his breakthrough film, *Putney Swope.* Courtesy: Jerry Ohlinger Archives.

After a while, the gags start being funny again because they simply do not quit. When the CEO of the ad agency dies of a stroke, stuttering in midsentence at the beginning of the film, the other board members at first think he's playing charades. Even after he's clearly dead, one of the executives (played by Joe Madden) endlessly shouts, "How many syllables, Mario?" Later in the film, when Putney is trying to come up with an angle for the Borman Six ads, one of his assistants repeatedly admonishes the other staff members, "Putney says the Borman Six girl has got to have *soul!*" and Downey's camera stares at him as the harangue continues for several minutes.

To play the president of the United States (President Mimeo) and the first lady, Downey cast a brother and sister Vaudeville team of dwarfs (Pepi and Ruth Hermine). "The president of the United States had to be a midget, for obvious reasons" (Downey). President Mimeo is jealous of Swope's success and wants to use Swope's talent to sell the Borman Six precisely because the car gets poor gas mileage and would thus boost oil consumption and profits. When threats fail, Mimeo attempts to approach Swope through Mark Focus (Eric Krupnik), a failed but arrogant photographer who yearns to work at the Truth and Soul agency. Mimeo suggests a "threesome" between Mark, Mimeo, and the first lady to get into Focus's good graces. The scene ends with the three tumbling into bed together, once again deliberately defying normative heterosexual behavior.

To give the film a stark, gray look, not unlike the world of advertising itself, Downey shot most of the film in subdued grays. Except for the raucous commercials supposedly produced by the Truth and Soul agency, which are filmed in suitably electric color, the film is photographed in black and white. The staged advertisements critique America's obsession with youth, whiteness, and the heterotopic couple. One ad, for Face Off pimple cream, is set in an idyllic pastoral landscape and features an interracial couple crooning at each other—as if in a Nelson Eddy–Jeanette MacDonald musical—about the virtues of the product they're pitching. Sample lyrics from the ad:

> You gave me a soul kiss
> It sure was grand
> You gave me a dry hump
> Behind the hot-dog stand.

It concludes with the refrain "My boyfriend's really out of sight / And so are his pimples." An air conditioner ad consists solely of a woman dancing suggestively down a slum alleyway toward the camera; the text advises the viewer, "You can't *eat* an air conditioner." An ad for Lucky Airlines depicts a passenger having slow-motion sex with the flight attendants as part of the regular service. In ridiculing the advertising profession's obsession with sex as a sales tool, as well as the audience to whom the ads cater, Downey emerged as a sexual satirist who wasn't afraid to conflate issues of race, sexuality, and commercial greed into one disruptive text. Financial backing for his next project was easy to obtain.

Downey's first major studio film, instead of being a topical satire, was the brooding, fatalistic *Pound* (1970) for United Artists (UA). It was also his son's debut as an actor. In *Pound,* a group of dogs, played by human beings without makeup, wait in the city animal shelter for adoption or execution. The film is a melancholy meditation on the nebulousness of contemporary existence and did little business at the box office. Ironically, one measure of Downey's hot status at the time was that no one at UA had bothered to read the script. When Downey turned in the first cut of the film, he was stunned to discover that UA executives had expected him to turn out a "feature-length animated cartoon" (Downey). Disappointed, UA finally put the film out as the bottom half of a double bill with Federico Fellini's *Satyricon* (1969), but the project's failure tarnished Downey's bankability with mainstream studios.

Fortunately, Downey received help for the next project from the private sector, in the form of a literal blank check from patron of the arts Cyma Rubin.

> [She] came to me and said, "What do you want to do next?" and I said, "Well, I have this thought about Christ coming back in a western," and she said, "I'll finance that," and she did, the whole budget. When the film was completed, she gave it to Cinema V to distribute. They didn't give her any money for it, but they took it over and put it in theaters and ran this huge ad in the *Village Voice* for the film, with one letter per full page, spelling out G-R-E-A-S-E-R-S-P-A-L-A-C-E. (Downey)

Greaser's Palace (1972) deals with the exploits of Jessy (Allan Arbus), a Christ figure who appears in the Wild West of 1880s America. He meets Vernon Greaser (James Antonio), a corrupt land baron, and his band of cutthroats, who hold court at Greaser's Palace, the saloon Vernon owns. Vernon runs the town with an iron hand; anyone who commits even a minor infraction is shot to death by Vernon or by his hired guns. The film opens with Vernon's wife, Cholero Greaser (the underappreciated Luana Anders), singing a dirgelike song praising virginity and condemning adultery to the loud applause of her husband. Although Cholero pretends to be faithful to Vernon, she seduces every man she can when he is away on business, thus making a mockery of the concept of connubial bliss. To impress Vernon and his gang, Jessy (who tells everyone that he is working for "the Agent Morris") performs a few pathetic miracles. Dressed in a zoot suit, he impresses no one until he displays stigmata on his hands; Downey's Christ figure is little more than a confused, two-bit showman. The Holy Ghost (Ronald Nealy) is presented as a nondescript man wearing a derby hat in a white sheet; his sole advice to Jessy is, "OK, kid, you're on." Vernon's son, Lamy "Homo" Greaser (Michael Sullivan), keeps getting fatally shot, knifed, and drowned by his father, only to be repeatedly raised by Jessy, Lazarus-like, from the dead. Toward the end of the film, Downey stages a touching father-and-son bonding scene in which Vernon finally accepts Lamy and tells him, "You're not a *homo;* you're a *greaser!*" The film concludes with the chronically constipated Vernon finally having a successful bowel movement, which blows up his desolate gambling house while a ragtag mariachi band plays on.

As he had done in *Putney Swope* and *Pound,* Downey continued to use often-baffling repetition humor in *Greaser's Palace.* Allan Arbus's Christ character continually asks, "What's going *down* here?" for no discernible reason. In another scene, a card shark tells Vernon Greaser, "Pick a card, any card . . . don't show it to me . . . now put it back in the deck. Is this the card?" "No," Greaser replies. "Is this the card?" "No." And on and on and on during a long tracking shot in the desert, for at least five minutes. Shot on location over seven weeks for eight hundred thousand dollars, *Greaser's Palace* added to Downey's maverick reputation, but the film failed to click at the box office (perhaps due to its cheerfully blasphemous theme), and Downey was once again looking for work.

Downey's next venture was a 1972 television adaptation of David Rabe's controversial anti–Vietnam War play *Sticks and Bones.* CBS Television backed the project sight unseen; it was produced by Joe Papp of the New York Shakespeare Festival and the Public Theatre. Amazingly, no one at CBS had ever heard of the play, nor had they bothered to read the screenplay, which was brutally critical of US involvement in Vietnam. One of the key texts that critiqued the United States' involvement in the Vietnam War, *Sticks and Bones* is a catalog of atrocities in which the concept of the "warrior male" is skillfully deconstructed. It is a direct response to such heteroperformative projects as *The Green Berets,* in which John Wayne sought to glorify the straight American soldiers who were drafted into the conflict, but also to marginalize those who opposed the war. CBS was not happy with the finished teleplay. Recalls Downey,

> [W]hen they first saw it, they panicked. They couldn't get anybody to buy any commercials, so it went out commercial-free. . . . CBS financed it because they thought, "If it's Joe Papp, it's gonna be Shakespeare," and they didn't even bother to read the thing. I liked it. And I liked that there were no commercials for two hours. (Downey)

Pound, Greaser's Palace, and *Sticks and Bones* marked Downey indelibly as an outsider, not one of the crowd; it was much the same position Preston Sturges found himself in during the latter stages of his career. Offers of work dried up. Intentionally or not, Downey had managed to alienate the Hollywood studios (with *Pound* for UA), independent producers (Cyma Rubin was reportedly disappointed that *Greaser's Palace* wasn't a greater financial success), and network television (CBS).

In 1980, Downey reluctantly accepted a gig as a writer on Chuck Barris's *Gong Show Movie* and later that same year agreed to direct the low-budget teen comedy *Up the Academy,* which failed to make a wave in the commercial marketplace. By his own admission, Downey hated making *Up the Academy* and was constantly at war with his producers during filming. Robert Downey, Sr. was stuck directing a series of films that he was, for one reason or another, unhappy with: *America* (shot in 1982, released in 1986); *Rented Lips* (1988), a bizarre comedy about two industrial filmmakers who get hoodwinked into directing a Nazi-themed porn film ("I really did that for Martin Mull" [Downey]); and the improvisational *Too Much Sun* (1991), with Robert Downey, Jr., Eric Idle, Howard Duff, and Andrea Martin, which failed to jell despite a promisingly tasteless premise (sister and brother must produce offspring to inherit a fortune; problem is, they're both gay). Meanwhile, Robert Downey, Jr. was rocketing to stardom as one of the 1980s and 1990s most bankable and mercurial stars.

Matters improved when Downey was able to find financing for *Hugo Pool* (1997), his most aesthetically successful project since *Putney Swope* and *Greaser's Palace*. Starring Alyssa Milano, Sean Penn, Malcolm McDowell, and—as Downey put it—"my kid," the film deals with the plight of a responsible, straight-ahead young woman (Milano, as Hugo Dugay of Hugo Pool), who must clean forty-five swimming pools in one day while dealing with her addict-alcoholic father, Henry Dugay (McDowell), and her casino-crazed mother, Minerva (Cathy Moriarty). The most satisfying part of the film is the relationship between Hugo and Floyd Gaylen (Patrick Dempsey), one of Hugo's customers. Confined to a wheelchair with amyotrophic lateral sclerosis (ALS), or Lou Gehrig's disease, Floyd still manages to form an intensely personal bond with Hugo that transcends his illness. The film was coscripted by Downey's second wife, Laura Ernst, who was suffering from ALS herself. Shortly after the completion of *Hugo Pool,* she died. *Hugo Pool* signaled a change in Downey's world-view: it was now both more accepting and less cynical. Typically, however, Downey does not pick a conventionally "desirable" couple for the romantic subplot of *Hugo Pool;* rather, he uses two individuals with serious problems who nevertheless find expression in each other, despite the barriers that society creates between them. The film is obviously autobiographical, but it makes the fictive heterosexual romance between Floyd and Hugo touching and believable.

Downey has also carved out a new career for himself as a character actor in *Boogie Nights* (1997), *Magnolia* (1999), and *To Live and Die in L.A.* (1985), and he worked on the script of a new film, "Forest Hills Bob." Interestingly, in the early 1980s, Downey tried to get a production of *The Talented Mr. Ripley* off the ground with his son in the role Matt Damon would eventually play (in 1999), but nothing came of it. Downey also began turning more of his attention to small-scale digital documentary projects to help other ALS sufferers. Looking back on his older films, Downey professes not to care about them, but a whole new generation of filmmakers clearly does. In a recent interview in the *Nation,* director Kasi Lemmons notes that, in the 1960s and 1970s, "there were a lot of really fabulous movies made . . . that were really, really powerful and would be extremely difficult to make now. I'm thinking of films that hardly get mentioned anymore, like . . . *Putney Swope*" (qtd. in Seymour 14).

Downey's vision is being taken up by a new generation of directors, including Jamie Babbit, whose film *But I'm a Cheerleader* (1999) was a

FIGURE 13. Jamie Babbit directing a scene from *But I'm a Cheerleader*. Courtesy: Jerry Ohlinger Archives.

breakout independent film hit. Babbit came to filmmaking through amateur theater and went on to direct a series of short films, including *Frog Crossing* (1996) and *The Sleeping Beauties* (1998), before making her debut as a feature director with *But I'm a Cheerleader*. Babbit stages *But I'm a Cheerleader* as a bright, popped-out comedy, with bright colors and heavily stylized sets. The film tells the story of femme Megan (Natasha Lyonne), a young woman who doesn't realize that she's a lesbian until her parents stage an intervention. Megan is shipped off to True Directions, a deprogramming center for gays and lesbians; there, they are forced to be straight. True Directions is run by the monstrously repressive Mary (Cathy Moriarty) and her in-denial gay son, Rock (Eddie Cibrian), with the assistance of camp supervisor Mike (played by RuPaul Charles in his first nondrag role). At True Directions, Megan meets and falls in love with the "butch" lesbian Graham (Clea DuVall), and despite all of Mary's threats and machinations, Megan and Graham's love triumphs.

Babbit's experience with actors allows her seamlessly to handle a large ensemble cast with practiced efficiency. She also works in television, where she directs the WB television series *Popular* and the MTV series *Undressed*. When I asked Babbit about the origins of *But I'm a Cheerleader*, she had this to say:

> I came to filmmaking through theater. I was born in Cleveland, Ohio, and I started at the Cleveland Playhouse when I was about seven years old, taking acting classes and then moving on to stage managing. There are a lot of elements of *Cheerleader* that are autobiographical. I never went to a homosexual "rehabilitation" camp, although such places do exist, like the Exodus Project, but my mother runs a treatment program for teenagers in Ohio called New Directions, which helps them beat alcohol and drug problems. My father is more like . . . Bud Cort['s] character in *Cheerleaders;* he's really sweet and supportive. He doesn't really want to talk about my being lesbian, but he's always been there for me. He's a lawyer. So I'd always wanted to do a comedy about growing up in rehab, and the absurdity of that atmosphere. But I didn't want to make fun of twelve-step programs for alcoholism and drugs because they really help people, but when you turn it into Homosexuals Anonymous, then I felt that was a situation I could have fun with.
>
> I came out to myself as a lesbian in high school, but it was one of those things that you kind of know, but you're not really sure, you know? I think I had lots of pictures of women in my locker at high school, just like the character of Megan in *Cheerleader*. (Babbit)

I remarked that the structure of *Cheerleader* seems to indicate an interest in performativity, defining gender through tasks: the boys play football, fix cars, chop wood, while the girls do household chores. It seems that the film is one enormous drag act, whether lesbian, heterosexual, or gay.

> I definitely wanted to talk about gender roles, gender expectations, and the absurdity of them, and I think a lot of that came from my own life. When I was coming out as a lesbian, a lot of people made fun of me because I was bad at sports[;] . . . one of the many bizarre gender expectations is that lesbians are supposed to be really good at sports. That's the kind of stuff I wanted to talk about in this film; how gender expectations define our lives and how others see us. In some ways, that's where the title of the film came from. Because Megan is a cheerleader, she can't believe that she's a lesbian. But then, at the end of the film, Megan uses her cheerleading skills to affirm her lesbian desire, when she urges Graham not to buckle under to the True Directions manifesto and [urges her] to come out as her lesbian lover. I didn't want it to be a film about a lesbian who comes out and then drives off on a motorcycle at the end. She was still a cheerleader at the end. (Babbit)

I asked Jamie how she would differentiate her film from such recent lesbian films as *Go Fish* (1994), *The Incredibly True Adventure of Two Girls in Love* (1995), *The Watermelon Woman* (1996), and *Boys Don't Cry* (1999), and her response was immediate.

> Well, they're told from the butch angle, and so they're films that I wouldn't make, but they're films that I like. But in *Cheerleader,* I wanted to make a conscious choice to have a femme protagonist. In *Go Fish,* Max is the femme character, but she's the love interest of Ely, the lead character, who gets the buzz cut. And when you deconstruct the film, Max becomes more butch, and that's how she gets the girl. And in *Incredibly True Adventure,* we're given a tomboy girl who ends up going for the femme, the object of her affections. In *Cheerleader,* I wanted the femme to be the pursuer, not the pursued. Not only movies, but also a lot of lesbian fiction I've read, a lot of lesbian narratives, are told from the butch perspective. And it was important to me to not tell that story again, because I wanted to show that a femme can be strong, and a femme can get what she wants.
>
> At the same time, one of the things I've been most interested in in the art world is the concept of "constructed realities," like Cindy Sherman, Red Grooms, Barbara Kruger—people who create an entire alternative

universe in which everything is hyperreal, popped out, colorful, and utterly plastic. So at the same time I wanted to talk about gender constructs and the absurdity of gender constructs, I wanted to explore the artifice and unreality of a completely constructed world in which nothing is real. I really wanted the sets and the world that I created for the characters in the film to be something unreal, campy, and yet really colorful and vibrant. Lots of pinks, blues, and very artificial. When I was going to Barnard, Red Grooms did an exhibit at Grand Central Station which I really loved; I adored his papier-mâché cityscapes. As part of this Grand Central exhibit, Grooms created a fake subway car that you could really sit down in, and it was like living inside a cartoon. That's the look I wanted for the film. I'm also really fond of Derek Jarman's work, particularly *Caravaggio* [1986] and *Queer Edward II* [1991], in which all of his sets are transparently constructed in one location. . . .

. . . [I]n the film *[But I'm a Cheerleader]*, True Directions is a really violent, horrible place, and I shot a lot of Cathy Moriarty's close-ups right in the camera, with a slight wide-angle lens to make her appear *really* scary. One of the things that I said to the production designer and the costume designer was that I wanted to be sure, as the film went on, that the materials for the sets and costumes became more artificial. So by the end, when all the kids at True Directions are "graduating" to the straight life in their plastic uniforms, I said, "I don't want cotton, I don't want polyester, I want pure plastic"—in the beginning, Megan's clothing is cotton; in the middle, polyester; and at the end, everything is entirely plastic. I wanted the production design and the sets to follow the same pattern because, at the end of the film, when the kids all say that they're "straight," that's the most artificial that they are; they're denying their true selves. In fact, everything that Cathy Moriarty wore was plastic from the beginning of the film to the end; the costume designers originally put her in a polyester uniform, and I said, "No, let's give her a plastic lab coat." I thought that her character should be really paranoid about diseases, AIDS, germs, and so we made everything sanitized. When she's outside cleaning her flowers, they're not even real flowers, because she doesn't believe in real sexual urges. To Mary, gay desire is unnatural, so let's go to a completely artificial place with her character.

I'm an optimist. I think it will be okay [to come out] because at least you will have love; Megan and Graham really love each other, and that love will carry them through a world full of problems and conflicts. The outside world may be hideous and horrible, and it may be a fight to stay alive, but if you have love, you'll be okay, no matter what happens[;] . . . the optimism of *Cheerleader* is one of the things that makes it something separate. Tim Burton and John Waters both go for the same kind of constructed, hyperreality that I use in my films, but they both have a darker edge to their work, and I'm more interested in using the camp aesthetic to make a positive statement. Then there's the whole question of women doing camp, which I don't think has ever really been done before. I wasn't interested in doing a camp movie that was completely satirical. I wanted it to have emotion, and I'm a romantic, so I wanted it to have some heart. (Babbit)

Babbit is at work on a new feature, "Conjugating Niki," in addition to continuing her work on *Popular* and *Undressed.* Babbit describes *Undressed* as being structured "just like a porn film—all the lead-ins, but no fucking," or sheer performativity (ritual body display and posing) without the sex act itself. Not surprisingly, most of the couples depicted on *Undressed* are resoundingly heterosexual, making Babbit's participation in the series both self-reflexive and deeply paradoxical. Babbit's work on *Undressed,* she made clear, is simply a matter of economic necessity, but as *But I'm a Cheerleader* readily demonstrates, Babbit can create an entirely believable world on a minimal budget (the film was shot for less than a million dollars). Babbit is at the beginning of her career, but in all her film work she offers a cheerful alternative to the dominant heterocentric cinema.

At the same time that Jamie Babbit has been constructing an alternative vision of the lesbian lifestyle in the United States, a group of young comics in Britain have been busily transforming the heterosexual-based television situation comedy into a zone of contested desire, socially disruptive violence, and grossly excessive heterosexual performativity. A variety of new British television shows, notably, *The Comic Strip, The Young Ones* (both of which briefly ran on MTV in the United States), *Absolutely Fabulous, The New Statesman,* and *Bottom* are being ravenously devoured by entranced viewers in Great Britain, although in the States they have been relegated to "cult" status. *Absolutely Fabulous,* chronicling the adventures of two middle-aged, utterly irresponsible, materialistic women and starring Jennifer Saunders and Joanna Lumley, managed to make a splash on the Comedy Central cable network in the United States. It features running gags of drunkenness, drug use, wretched excess, and capitalistic greed. Saunders, the creator of the series, oversaw a series of episodes that were at once universally accessible and wittily engaging to audiences in both the United States and Britain, reveling in broad slapstick and cheerfully vulgar humor. All of these series feature sledgehammer violence, increased doses of vulgarity, and a savage brutality that lampoons every last remaining remnant of the empire's decaying colonialist social fabric. No one has embraced this new approach as fervently as Rik Mayall and Adrian Edmondson, whose *Bottom* series became an instant sensation when broadcast by that last bastion of cultural respectability, the BBC. (Edmondson, incidentally, is married to *Absolutely Fabulous*'s Jennifer Saunders.)

Adrian Edmondson and Rik Mayall met at Manchester University as students and formed an undergraduate comedy act, the Dangerous Brothers. In essence, their act consisted of violent slapstick comedy—reminiscent of the Three Stooges—in which two perpetually feuding arrested adolescents, Richie Dangerous (Mayall) and Sir Adrian Dangerous (Edmondson), attempt to kill each other with various kitchen implements and other household items; they inflicted grievous bodily harm upon each other, without any real long-term consequences. The duo eventually brought the Dangerous Brothers to late-night British television, until the cheerfully mordant skits were banned due to excessive violence and bad taste. At the same time, Mayall and Edmondson began making nightclub appearances at various local venues, including the Comedy Store in London. In 1980, Edmondson cofounded the comedy troupe the Comic Strip, serving as actor and writer, at the Boulevard Theatre (whose routine evolved into the successful television series).

In 1982, Mayall and Edmondson cocreated the hit show *The Young Ones,* which parodied an early 1960s heterotopic romance film starring British pop star Cliff Richard. The series, which ran from 1982 to 1984, was a further extension of the pair's violent brand of domestic comedy—in this case it chronicled the misadventures of four college students living together in a state of perpetual filth and penury, and was punctuated (naturally) with marathon bouts of brutal physical comedy. *The Young Ones* led to a series of episodes of *The Comic Strip* on television and a savage television satire entitled *The New Statesman,* in which Mayall portrayed Alan B'Stard, a vicious Tory politician who relentlessly schemes, swindles, and connives his way to fame and fortune. This series, which lasted from 1987 to 1994, firmly established Mayall as one of the most energetic and outrageous members of the new school of British comedy. At the same time Mayall was teaming with Edmondson on the *Bottom* teleseries, which chalked up eighteen episodes on the BBC between 1991 and 1995.

In this period, the busy pair also appeared in a variety of touring theatrical presentations (including *Hooligan's Island*). Edmondson also
directed several rock videos and participated in a host of other writing, performing, and theatrical ventures, including a well-received revival of
Samuel Beckett's *Waiting for Godot* in 1991 at the Queen's Theatre in London (in which Edmondson and Mayall costarred). This unrelenting spate
of activity came to an abrupt halt when Mayall was nearly killed in a freak
motorcycle accident in April 1998 near his home in the English countryside. Mayall's recovery was long and painful, but by 1999, Mayall and
Edmondson were once again ready to embark upon a new venture, one
that would push their brand of social criticism to a new level: *Guest House
Paradiso,* a feature film that Mayall and Edmondson cowrote and that
Edmondson directed. In a sense, everything that Edmondson and Mayall
had been working up to is encapsulated in this film, which is a brilliant
and unremittingly savage attack on the crumbling façade of the British
leisure industry and the myth of the happily married heterotopic couple.

Guest House Paradiso takes as its central situation the premise that, in
some peculiar fashion, Eddie and Richie have come into possession of a
spectacularly run-down guesthouse located at the edge of a cliff in the
English countryside. It is conveniently situated next to a malfunctioning
nuclear power plant. The guesthouse has only one or two permanent res-
idents, most notably Mrs. Foxfur (Fenella Fielding), a vague, rich, and
aging client from whom Eddie and Richie attempt to extort additional
rooming fees on a nearly daily basis. The only other guests are the members of the aptly named Nice family, Mr. and Mrs. Nice (Simon Pegg and
Lisa Palfrey) and their children, Damien (Joseph Hughes) and Charlene
(Jessica Mann). The Nices are impossibly clean, freshly scrubbed, and
utterly heteronormative in their sexual preferences—they are straightness
personified. In contrast, Richie and Eddie's sadomasochistic relationship
is a bizarre mixture of ritual battery, verbal abuse, and ultimately stoic
acquiescence—they make up a typically dysfunctional old married couple. While nominally heterosexual, they are clearly not part of the normative straight world inhabited by the Nices and their two picture-per-
fect children. Richie, an insecure martinet, treats the Nice family as a
pestilence to be eradicated as quickly and as conveniently as possible.
Eddie, who is more of a romantic and less abrasive, seems dimly aware of
the opposite sex, and yet his unkempt wardrobe and lack of social skills
keep him safely beyond the reach of any genuine heterosexual liaison.

Upon arriving at Guest House Paradiso for their "dream vacation," the Nice family are aghast at the decrepit nature of their accommodations but, as Mr. Nice informs his wife and children, "[T]his is the cheapest guest house in all of England, and it's all we can afford, so we'll just have to make the best of it." As the Nice children repair to the children's play area (strategically located at the edge of the cliff) for a nearly fatal round on the swing set, "internationally famous" Italian film star Gina Carbonara (Hélène Mahieu) arrives incognito, hoping to throw the pursuing paparazzi off her trail. She, in turn, is followed by her jilted lover, the outrageously macho Gino Bolognese (Vincent Cassel), who will do anything to retain Gina's affection. In all of this, Richie Twat ("It's pronounced *thwaite*," he continually insists in vain) and the slow-witted Eddie Elizabeth Ndingombaba (Mayall and Edmondson, respectively) retain their air of bumbling incompetence (Eddie) and sneering pomposity (Richie). To keep costs down, they force their guests to eat, for the main dinner entrée, radioactive fish that have washed up on the beach; meanwhile, they rob the guests of whatever valuables they may possess, even as they remain completely oblivious to all client complaints. The film concludes with a marathon vomiting sequence in which all of the hotel's guests fall seriously ill, courtesy of the nuclear cuisine, although only the putative villain of the piece, Gino, dies as a result of this poisoning.

Just as it looks as if Richie and Eddie's entire investment in the guest house will be forfeited due to their incompetence, greed, and thievery, a top-secret deputation from the British government (which is apparently even more corrupt than either Richie or Eddie) arrives with two gigantic suitcases stuffed with hundred-pound notes. They offer the pair the money and asylum on a tropical isle if they will only sign a document that attests (in part) that they have "never been in England, or even *heard* the word *radioactivity.*" Without a moment's hesitation, Richie and Eddie sign, and the film ends with the pair comfortably ensconced in the lap of primitive luxury in the tropics (very much like an old Bing Crosby–Bob Hope *Road* picture).

Some reviewers have compared the film to episodes of the John Cleese teleseries *Fawlty Towers,* and although there is a superficial resemblance, this is only part of the equation. The centerpiece of *Guest House Paradiso* is first, last, and always violent slapstick, and Richie and Eddie's motivations throughout the film are never—not for a second—honorable. One abortive scheme leads to another, all in a mad quest for personal and selfish gain. Both men are devoid of even a single sympathetic trait. It's *not* all in good fun for Richie and Eddie, who owe no allegiance to anyone, not even to each other.

The major set piece of *Guest House Paradiso* (a set piece that is craftily exploited in the trailer for the film) is an unbelievably brutal fight in the hotel's kitchen while Richie and Eddie are ostensibly engaged in preparing food for their unfortunate guests. Although domestic mayhem is a staple of the *Bottom* series, as well as *The Young Ones,* here, with a generous budget and the ability to stage some truly spectacular stunts, Edmondson and Mayall stage an all-out war that rivals anything offered up by the Three Stooges, Charlie Chaplin, or Harold Lloyd. In addition, near the beginning of the film, in a sequence that is reminiscent of Buster Keaton's memorable stunts, Edmondson performs a series of truly astounding maneuvers on a motorcycle. He falls asleep at the wheel, only to crash into the front of the hotel and, through an intricate series of pratfalls, he winds up behind the hotel's front desk as if nothing had happened, ready to receive visitors.

While Edmondson is clearly the more dominant member of the team (Edmondson dreams up most of the gags, much as Stan Laurel was the more creative member of the Laurel and Hardy team), Mayall serves as the perfect foil for all this carefully staged mayhem, with a fine sense of direct, no-nonsense craftsmanship. For his part, Edmondson has gone to great lengths to dismiss any speculation that *Guest House Paradiso* might be anything more than a commercial entertainment. He also downplays his considerable skill as a director, commenting, "If you've written the idea then directing's not a big thing, getting lots of people to do what you want to do" (qtd. in Wills). But in its vicious, violent, raucous, no-holds-barred approach to such issues as class warfare, the decaying hold of the British empire, and the sexual mechanics of forced social heteroperformativity, *Guest House Paradiso* recalls such classic British comedies as *The Lavender Hill Mob* (1951), *The Ladykillers* (1955), and *The Belles of St. Trinian's* (1954), all of which were considered merely commercial entertainments when first released.

The vulgarity of *Guest House Paradiso* is mostly in the language, which is on par with the more extravagant excesses of television's *South Park,* coupled with the sneering arrogance of Mayall's upper-class character and the seeming stupidity of Edmondson as his comic foil. Many of the most memorable gags in the film operate simultaneously at the level

FIGURE 14. Rik Mayall *(left, cowering)* and Adrian Edmondson *(right, brandishing fire extinguisher)* attempt to settle their differences amicably in *Guest House Paradiso*. Courtesy: Ronald Grant Archive.

of stupidity and genius, as is the case with the candle-in-the-eye gag, which is used when Eddie and Richie are struggling through an extremely narrow crawlspace on their way to a guest's room to steal (without any compunction whatsoever) some of the guests' belongings. At a particularly inopportune moment, Richie drops the candle and, in an attempt to retrieve it, accidentally sticks the still-flaming candle in his right eye. Shrieking with pain, he tries to explain to Eddie what's happened. "Candle in the eye!" he exclaims, but dimwitted Eddie is baffled. *"Candle in the eye!"* Richie screams. Eddie responds with a bemused shrug and obligingly sticks the still-lit candle in Richie's *left* eye. A gag like this is both obvious and transcendent in its embrace of surreal stupidity; while the entire premise is preposterous, as a piece of slapstick the joke is deftly executed, even as the audience winces in pain at Richie's predicament.

Eddie and Richie have a decidedly uneven relationship with one another. Richie is brash, rude, snide, and repellent; he is an upper-class twit without any real intellectual or social credentials to back him up. Eddie is the slow camp follower, forever the object of Richie's verbal abuses, to which he can only reply with outbursts of infantile, inarticulate violence. Just as Moe Howard in the Three Stooges seemed to live in a state of perpetual irritation, while Curly bumbled from one violent accident to another—further arousing Moe's ever present wrath—(Larry Fine being the blankly agreeable go-between), Richie and Eddie represent the twin halves of arrested male heterosexual adolescence at their most immature and childish. They are figures which the audience can safely look down upon. If Richie is the consummate social parasite and obsequious flatterer, Eddie is the average, somewhat vague character who does his best to cope with the chaos around him, chaos often caused by his own incompetence and/or Richie's false dreams of grandiose superiority. Combining youthful aggressiveness with a string of undesirable character traits (laziness, greed, unrestrained anger, jealousy—the list is nearly endless), Richie and Eddie represent the worst possible outcome of a British public school education and are thus exemplars of a society in collapse.

Most refreshing in the narrative and in the imagistic construction of *Guest House Paradiso* is its scrupulous lack of misogyny and sexism, which is one of the many things that makes the film's vision unique in mainstream cinema. Gina Carbonara's character is never demeaned or exploited; there are none of the sniggering burlesque jokes associated with *The Benny Hill Show* or with the later, less interesting *Carry On* films. Of all the characters in the film, only Gino Bolognese, whose personality itself is a compound criticism of the worst aspects of typical macho heterosexual behavior, comes to a deservedly bad end, after attempting to rape Gina—an assault instinctively prevented by Richie and Eddie because such things simply *aren't acceptable.* A free-for-all in the kitchen is one thing, but despite the continual mayhem, no one is in any real danger of getting hurt. Gina's character is never called upon to do a nude scene, and even the elderly and somewhat senile Mrs. Foxfur (although she is punched unconscious by Richie, who then futilely attempts to dig the gold out of her teeth with a pickax) usually gets the best of Richie and Eddie and escapes any real harm or indignity. This is, after all, a *cartoon.* Otherwise, as Richie notes, in a direct address to the spectator at the end of the film, the narrative's structure "would be morally questionable."

In the world of *Guest House Paradiso,* everyone exists to be ridiculed, especially the Nice family (whose only "crime" is that they are too conventional, too representative of the heterocentric family unit), but the innocence and genuine humanity represented by Gina Carbonara is the moral center of the film and counterbalances the excess of violence that surrounds her. Gina comes to the guest house seeking sanctuary from the pressures of fame, and she receives it, along with the assistance of Richie and Eddie in extricating herself from the unwanted attentions of Gino (who at one point demands that two prostitutes share his bed with Gina in a moment reminiscent of Lord Byron's wedding night). One could easily argue that this strategy of feminine purity harkens back to the many women in Chaplin's films (*City Lights* [1931], *The Gold Rush* [1925], and *Modern Times* [1936] being prime examples), and yet when one compares Gina's treatment in *Guest House Paradiso* to the continual indignities suffered by Carol Cleveland in the *Monty Python* teleseries or by Margaret Dumont in the Marx Brothers films, it seems that Richie and Eddie have constructed in *Guest House Paradiso* a comic ethos that is a decided departure from the grinding exploitation to which women in comic films are routinely subjected. As Fenella Fielding (Mrs. Foxfur) noted in an on-camera interview during the making of the film, "I don't *think* I've ever been punched in the eye before in a film, although of course they didn't *actually* hit me. But they were such *gentlemen* about it" (*Making of* Guest House Paradiso).

The technical expertise displayed in the film is another point of interest. Unlike the slack comedic structure that one finds in such recent

American films as *Dumb and Dumber* (1994), *Deuce Bigalow: Male Gigolo* (1999), *Big Daddy* (1999), and others of this ilk (all of which are also marred by a conspicuous streak of forced sentimentality), *Guest House Paradiso* is a model example of economy in construction, brevity of running time, and meticulous care in execution. Gags and pratfalls are executed with split-second timing and are edited together with seamless precision; the narrative pacing of the film is never allowed to slacken, as Eddie and Richie race from one misadventure to the next. If *Guest House Paradiso* offends the mainstream critics, one should recall that the *Carry On* films in the late 1950s and early 1960s were also critically reviled, precisely because they pushed past the boundaries of what was then considered good taste. With its sledgehammer comedy, brutal cartoon violence, and, most tellingly, its accurate lampooning of the last frayed remnants of the British social and heterosexual fabric, *Guest House Paradiso* gestures toward a new and more direct form of comedic address, which audiences on the Continent fervently embrace. *Guest House Paradiso* suggests that whatever artificial barriers might have remained in filmic comedy have been effectively shattered, that a new breed of "hyperreal" slapstick can be effectively melded with a narrative line that both develops the characters and their world and sustains the audience's interest. Now that the barricades have fallen, what will happen next? Further assaults by Richie, Eddie, and their compatriots on the public decency are certainly to be expected (a sequel is in the works), and as *Guest House Paradiso* persuasively demonstrates, such escapades are essential to the vibrancy and vitality of film comedy, as well as to the fabric of any open society, and are therefore eminently desirable. British comedies, such as *Guest House Paradiso* and the *Carry On* series, offer a zone of chaotic dystopia that effectively undermines staid notions of the status quo, including heterosexuality and the nuclear family.

CHAPTER FOUR

✖

The Commodification of Straightness

As contemporary filmmakers push performative sexual display into a new realm of specificity, they also seek to recreate, rather than repeat, the past. These recreations are often tinged with the unreliable patina of nostalgia and collective memory. The recent wave of World War II films, for an obvious example, memorializes both a conflict and a social regime now beyond the zone of accurate recall. As Tom Carson argues,

> Lusting after bygone luster, Americans now pine for World War II as if it's an Eden from which we've been exiled. What both explains the hyperbole and accounts for its desperate undertone is that the memory of the war is slipping away from us, with only a dwindling number of people still able to recall it firsthand. (32)

In the heterosexual love triangle in the film *Pearl Harbor* (2001), Ben Affleck and Josh Hartnett are locked in a romantic triangle with Kate Beckinsale; while the director, Michael Bay, seeks to foreground their conflicted romance, using the attack as a backdrop. The hyperspectacularized scenes of destruction and violence that dominate the film become *Pearl Harbor*'s most authoritative text. As Carson notes, "Bay is the leading light of the steamroller school of high-tech filmmaking that one critic has labeled 'post-human'" (21), and in its carefully constructed digital shipboard explosions and sequences of aerial attack, *Pearl Harbor* is more a synthetic project than a historical investigation. But as Carson points out,

131

the story of *Pearl Harbor,* as with any event, depends on who is telling the tale. Describing a Japanese version of the attack that launched the United States' entry into World War II in earnest, Carson writes,

> As dawn breaks, the pilots tie on their ceremonial head scarves. Moments later, their planes hurtle off the carrier's deck, cheered by superior officers waving their hats in dignified circles and by mechanics whose jubilation is less restrained. Then comes the attack, which is a howling success. As his aircraft banks away from the ruins of the enemy's battleship fleet, the hero reminisces in wistful voice-over: "What a wonderful day!"
>
> Needless to say, this isn't the climax of "Pearl Harbor," the coming Hollywood spectacular about the most famous sneak attack in United States history. It's the opening sequence of a Japanese film called "I Bombed Pearl Harbor.". . . "I Bombed Pearl Harbor" was released in the United States in 1960 [sic], in a dubbed version that was doubtless recut. . . . Although clumsy, the movie is often fascinating, since the Japanese, for understandable reasons, didn't make many World War II epics—not for export, anyway. Every movie buff knows that the losers dealt with the horrific finale of Hiroshima and Nagasaki by inventing Godzilla instead. (21)

One can look at both films as commercials for the ideological construct of World War II, with various racial, social, and sexual codes being revived and presented to the audience. The Japanese film stresses duty, valor, and honor above all other considerations; it presents a hypermasculinized vision of warfare as the proving ground for performed heterosexual manhood. American versions, by contrast, including not only *Pearl Harbor* but also *Tora! Tora! Tora!* (1970), *In Harm's Way* (1965), *From Here to Eternity* (1953), and numerous other films that document this period in history, inevitably find a way to weave a dominant theme of heterocentric romance (or at least, contestation) into the film's overarching narrative. What is being sold here, as in such anticommunist hysteria films as *The Iron Curtain* (1948), *The Red Menace* (1949), *I Married a Communist* (1949), *The Whip Hand* (1951), *Big Jim McLain* (1952), *Rocket Attack, U.S.A.* (1961), and other films of the mid to late 1950s (when the implied threat of communist domination had replaced the more tangible threat of the Axis powers of World War II), was the commodification of a way of life continually threatened by forces that sought to destabilize it (Barson and Heller 74–83). America's consumer culture is based on the premise that one can purchase one's freedom, bit

FIGURE 15. Images of winged victory in *I Bombed Pearl Harbor*. Courtesy: Jerry Ohlinger Archives.

by bit, at ever larger, more impersonal warehouse stores, such as Wal-Mart, Kmart, Home Depot, and other giant retail chains that masquer-ade as hometown exponents of capitalism but that are in reality expo-nents of corporate and cultural dominance, every bit as pervasive as any external ideological regime.

In the 1950s, women in particular were told that, since homemaking was to be their inevitable and inescapable career role, they would have to purchase the correct attire for their forthcoming role. They should look the part with confidence. The 1955 text *Homemaking for Teen-agers,* for example, asks its female readers, "Do You Have Clothes Sense?"

> Did you realize that how you dress and how much you spend for clothing is one of your homemaking responsibilities? Naturally you wish to make a good appearance for your own sake, but also for the sake of your family. This does not mean that you should dress expensively or elaborately. Indeed, you can be well dressed on a small budget if you know how to choose the right clothes for your needs, how to select attractive and becoming clothing, and [how] to get good value for your money. These are things you must learn in order to have good *clothes sense!* (McDermott and Nicholas 436)

As Brian Swimme notes, it is the ad industry's desire to make the viewer *unhappy* with his or her present condition, whether it be clothing, furniture, food, car, job, or any other commodifiable aspect of one's exis-tence. This conditioning starts at the cradle and continues until the day of one's death.

> Advertisements are where our children receive their cosmology, their basic grasp of the world's meaning, which amounts to their primary "faith," though they don't recognize it as such. Perhaps the more recalci-trant children will view upwards of a hundred thousand ads before they cave in and accept consumerism's basic worldview. But eventually they all get the message. It's a simple cosmology, told to great effect and delivered a billion times a day, not only to Americans, but to nearly everyone on the planet. Its message: *human beings exist to work at jobs, to earn money, to buy stuff.* (Swimme 19)

This thought is amplified in *Adbusters* magazine by a writer who astutely comments that, in today's consumer society, shopping is "the only adven-ture left" ("Privatopia" 31–32). This leads to a loss of personal space, as one's being becomes not a separate social unit but part of a vast, ever-consuming public, desiring only the acquisition of more goods in a desperate search for happiness and fulfillment. This search is only momentarily assuaged by the purchase of a given item, before the inevitable quest for the next object kicks in.

> There are a lot of security guards inside the Mall of America [MOA] in Bloomington, Minnesota, but then, no one's going to steal your kids there, or ask you to help break up a fist fight. The Mall of America is 78 acres of parking lots, consumer junk, and *psychological relief.* Try to imagine what it would feel like to be at the center of 78 acres of tropical rainforest, or to walk through 78 acres of Calcutta, and you'll understand the attraction of the MoA. Here, adventure begins when a woman in the pith helmet sitting on a plastic elephant calls your "safari" into the Rainforest Café. They call mall space "quasi public," and it leads to an inevitable question: Why ever leave? (29)

More to the point, how *can* one leave? The plastic perfection of the MoA extends far beyond its putative borders and into the consciousness of corporate American culture, seeking to present life without risk or danger, relationships without pain or growth, and most of all the reassurance that, as a member of a heterocentric society, one is part of the ruling elite, which shapes both the desires of and the models for contemporary society.

When challenges to the straight, white, dominant social order emerged in the late 1940s in such disruptive film noir classics as *Accomplice* (1946), *Apology for Murder* (1945), *Backlash* (1947), *Shock* (1946), *Decoy* (1946), *The Mysterious Mr. Valentine* (1946), and other postwar films of disillusionment (see Lyons 67–162), contemporary audiences were simultaneously repelled and enthralled by the spectacle presented to them: American society, fresh from victory in World War II, in complete moral and social collapse. In *Shock,* the wife of a returning veteran accidentally witnesses a murder committed by the head of a mental institution (played by Vincent Price). The doctor, with the help of his heterodystopian love interest (Lynn Bari), subjects the unfortunate woman to nearly fatal insulin-shock therapy in a vain attempt to erase her memory or, failing that, to kill her. Only the last-minute intervention of the wife's rather gullible husband prevents her murder, and Price kills himself in disgrace. In *Shock,* as in most film noir, all authority is counterfeit, all social agencies corrupt. Most intriguing in *Shock* is the final triumph (however contrived) of the husband and wife, whose bond of heterosexual love is privileged by the film's narrative over that of the scheming psychiatrist and his mistress. True noirs, especially *Detour* (1945) and *Scarlet Street* (1945), end on a note of unrelieved pessimism, but who is to say that closure is proved within the scope of the film's narrative alone? Straight patrons exiting a theater after seeing *Detour* could comfort themselves with the assertion that, despite the moral vacuum inhabited by the film's characters, the observable world of the viewer remains tranquil and predictable. Closure for all fictive narratives is located not within the work itself but in the circumstances of one's own existence.

Seen in this light, all dystopian or utopian narratives remain subject to modification by the realm of our actual lives, as interpreted and/or modified by the roles we play, the clothes we wear, the beliefs and value systems we subscribe to, and our status within (or without) society. As Jean Baudrillard notes in *The Illusion of the End*, "[M]anaging the end therefore becomes synonymous with the management of catastrophe" (66), the ways in which the viewer mediates spectacular disaster *(Pearl Harbor)* or personal breakdown *(Detour).* All the endings provided to us by fictive constructs are not conclusions but momentary resting places, just as the heterosexualization of products, rather than people, remains the dominant commodity of new millennial commercial discourse. "We have dehumanized sex, and then sexualized everything else—from airline travel to soft drinks," notes Quentin Crisp in *Manners from Heaven* (66), and this omnipresent reconfiguration of the straight landscape into a zone of absent desire informs not only the commerce but also the interpersonal relationships of the average American social consumer. The standardization of all aspects of existence—chain restaurants, chain theaters, enormous warehouse-style shopping centers—coupled with a concomitant standardization of design, makes the consumer feel secure, safe, and satisfied within certain carefully prescribed limits. The standardized image of consumerism that mushroomed in the 1950s above all gave expression to a desire to belong to a unified field, a social system in which one might recognize one's self in others. When architecture was unable to contain social disruptiveness, employees of restaurants, stores, and businesses were required to extend this conformity to their manner of dress. In the car-friendly 1950s, drive-in restaurants became nearly ubiquitous.

> Since the drive-in's atmosphere could not be firmly regulated through the design and décor of an interior dining room, it became all the more important to have carhops maintain an agreed-upon standard of dress and behavior: in the customer's mind, the carhops rather than the architecture epitomized the drive-in's character. (Langdon 64)

The standardization, then, of fast-food architecture coincided with the standardization of heterosexuality as the sole normative form of social and sexual discourse, as exemplified by the uniformity of the personnel. For a short time in the 1960s, the ready availability of contraception, coupled with a disenchantment with the mores of the Eisenhower era, caused consumers to reconsider their dedication to one uniform model for everyone. However, the "aggressive experimentation with modern forms" (Langdon 97) that typified not only early-1960s architecture but also radical sexual experimentation dimmed as the wave of assassinations and the Vietnam War sapped the energy for cultural change from the national collective consciousness by the early 1970s.

Director Howard Hawks, who created an early prototype of the self-sufficient female protagonist in his films *Only Angels Have Wings* (1939), *His Girl Friday* (1940), *Red River* (1948), and numerous other hyperheterosexualized films, commented in an interview near the end of his life,

> I've been accused of promoting Women's Lib, and I've denied it, emphatically. It just happens that kind of a woman is attractive to me. I merely am doing somebody that I like. And I've seen so many pictures where the hero gets in the moonlight and says silly things to a girl, I'd reverse it and let the girl do the chasing around, you know, and it works out pretty well. . . . I'd much rather work with a character like that than with some little Puritan violet. (qtd. in McBride 96)

Indeed, the creation of the Hawksian woman was only one of the director's innovations. He cast the obviously gay Montgomery Clift against John Wayne in *Red River* and counted on the conscientiousness of Clift's method acting to stand as an effective contrast to Wayne's no-nonsense heterosexual performativity; he teamed Humphrey Bogart and Lauren Bacall in *To Have and Have Not* (1944) and *The Big Sleep* (1946; a 1945 version is now available) as lovers who are insolent equals; he directed the bisexual Cary Grant in one of the most commercially successful drag comedies ever made, *I Was a Male War Bride* (1948); and he cast Rock Hudson as a bumbling outdoorsman in *Man's Favorite Sport?* (1964), effectively burlesquing Hudson's ultra-hetero screen image. Yet for all of his transgressiveness, Hawks was, at his core, completely homophobic. When asked,

> *What do you think when critics say, as some in fact have, that the male characters in your films border on homosexuality?*
> [He responded,] I'd say it's a goddam silly statement to make. It sounds like a homosexual speaking. (McBride 147)

Nor did Hawks have much use, somewhat surprisingly, for any variations on the John Wayne mold of performative heterosexuality in his films. "Most of the leading men today, the younger men especially, are a little bit effeminate. There's no toughness. [Steve] McQueen and [Clint] Eastwood don't compare with Wayne" (116). Ultimately, for Howard Hawks, the realm of performative sexuality has dominion over all other social or sexual constructs. It is clear that Hawks saw homosexuality as a threat. In much the same manner, Americans saw the threat of communism blown up into a mass frenzy in the early 1950s, and the nation saw the eruption of gays and lesbians into mainstream culture (after decades of living on the margins of society, excoriated by social guardians and arbiters of contemporary mores) as a challenge (rather than as an alternative) to mainstream, heterosexual society.

It is no accident that public fascination with extraterrestrial beings also erupted in the 1950s and continues to the present, uneasy day. Hawks's production of *The Thing from Another World* (1951) presents audiences with a carnivorous, highly intelligent plant that drains the living of their blood to survive; *Invisible Invaders* (1959) depicts an attack of human corpses that have been reanimated by aliens, which are bent upon conquering Earth by any means possible; *Earth vs. the Flying Saucers* (1956) depicts Washington, DC, under siege by disc-shaped UFOs; *The Mysterians* (1957) deals with men from a dying planet who seek to abduct the women of Earth for breeding purposes (Nesheim and Nesheim 70–82). All of these threats, perceived and actual, articulate the distress of a social order that is undergoing rapid change from within and that is seeking to suppress this disruptive discourse by presenting it as simultaneously seductive and dangerous, a menace to the status quo.

FIGURE 16. American machismo: Howard Hawks and John Wayne, with Michele Carey *(back to camera)*, shooting Hawks's *El Dorado* on the streets of Old Tucson. Courtesy: Jerry Ohlinger Archives.

Even in the blandest 1950s entertainments, the social order is constantly being called into question. In *Gidget* (1959), Sandra Dee is more interested in surfing than in dating boys (Doherty, *Teenagers* 197); and teens of that era decisively rejected such utterly antiseptic films as *Hound-Dog Man* (1959), a tepid romance starring Fabian, despite a desperate campaign to retain "normative heterosexual" values launched on the film's behalf (television's *American Bandstand* even ran a "Why I Would Like a Date with Fabian" contest, to no avail [Doherty, *Teenagers* 214]). Much more enticing were such exotic confections as *I Was a Teenage Werewolf* and *I Was a Teenage Frankenstein* (both 1957), which offered teen audiences the vicarious opportunity to strike back at the teachers, policemen, and other authority figures who continually harassed them while simultaneously delivering to the increasingly jaded, voyeuristic teens stepped-up doses of sex and violence. Stephen King expressed his disgust with the "clean teen" films of the 1950s (which he endured as a youth), noting,

> During *The Parent Trap* [1961], I kept hoping Hayley Mills would run into Vic Morrow from *The Blackboard Jungle* [1955]. That would have livened things up a little, by God. I felt that one look at Vic's switchblade knife and gimlet gaze would have put Hayley's piddling domestic problems in some kind of reasonable perspective. And when I lay in bed at night under my eave, listening to the wind in the trees or the rats in the attic, it was not Debbie Reynolds as Tammy or Sandra Dee as Gidget that I dreamed of, but Yvette Vickers from *Attack of the Giant Leeches* [1959] or Luana Anders from *Dementia 13* [1963]. Never mind sweet; never mind uplifting; never mind Snow White and the Seven Goddam Dwarfs. At thirteen I wanted monsters that ate whole cities, radioactive corpses that came out of the ocean and ate surfers, and girls in black bras who looked like trailer trash. (45)

But in all heterocentric entertainment, the man has one primary responsibility: he must defer, or seem to defer, to the object of his affections. Writing in the "men's" magazine *Esquire* in 1962, Paul Gallico advised his male readers, "[I]f you want to live in a happy, peaceful world, then you must arrange to keep the women satisfied" (219); "let's face it—the main object of your getting together with a woman is somehow to satisfy your libido, yet find a mate with whom you can live *bloodlessly*" (224; my emphasis). In *Soylent Green* (1973), a dystopic science-fiction film in which the bodies of the newly dead are ground up into food pellets to feed the starving citizens of a direly overpopulated planet, women are referred to quite frankly as "furniture" but, Gallico seems to suggest, like a chair or a table, they are still necessary for every heterosexual home. As in Jim Thompson's preferred form of fiction writing, the first-person confessional (in such films as *Diary of a High School Bride* [1959], *College Confidential* [1960], and *Sorority Girl* [1957]), sex is a site of negotiation, contestation, and secrecy, where one's desires, to be satiated, must first be articulated. As Michel Foucault notes in *The History of Sexuality,*

> If it was necessary to extract the truth of sex through the technique of confession, this was not simply because it was difficult to tell, or stricken by the taboos of decency, but because the ways of sex were obscure; it was elusive by nature; its energy and its mechanisms escaped observation, and its causal power was partly clandestine. (*Introduction* 66)

This clandestine force could not be brought forth with direct enunciation; myriad alternative routes were required to reach the surface of one's consciousness. Thus heterosexually based negotiations in the 1950s were essentially a private affair, involving only the couple involved in their ultimate ritual performative display and enactment. A certain amount of bare-chested female performative ritualization became an expected glyph of the exploitation (and later the mainstream) films of the 1970s; the stakes have risen with each successive decade, until the production of such films as *Romance* (1999) and *Baise-moi* (2000) frankly commingle all aspects of gay and straight play within the constructions of their narratives, creating by their production a new audience demand for complete bodily display and/or rupture as an intrinsic part of the spectacle being presented. And yet, despite their seemingly limitless graphic specificity, the intensely sexualized spectacle presented in *Romance* and *Baise-moi* is finally as inauthentic and as constructed as the most repressive films of the 1950s—a phantasmal exhibition of virtual bodies, anchored only in the realm of performance.

Artists in the 1960s—performance artists Yayoi Kusama and Yoko Ono, and filmmaker Ben Van Meter, for example—presented a new vision of the performative sexual body without conventional censorship. In Kusama's "Grand Orgy to Awaken the Dead at MOMA," a group of performers disrobed in the pond of the Museum of Modern Art's sculpture garden, on 25 August 1969; Yoko Ono staged "bed-ins" with John Lennon; and filmmaker Ben Van Meter's epic experimental film, *Acid*

Mantra: Rebirth of a Nation (1966–68), presented long sections of heterosexual lovemaking in a bucolic California commune. But although these films and performance pieces were highly influential and widely screened and performed in the artistic underground around the globe, their impact on mainstream cinema was more subtle. It took a long time for the directness of address espoused by these artists to reach the general public. At the same time, the purity of purpose and execution in experimental films of the 1960s was inevitably cheapened and coarsened by the time commercial filmmakers incorporated these new standards into their works; performative heterosexuality was adulterated by links to violence, drugs, and spiritual nihilism. At the same time, such pioneer artists as Ron Rice, Andy Warhol, and Jack Smith were fashioning a gay alternative to the stultifying grip of heterotopia in their films—*The Flower Thief* (1960), *The Chelsea Girls* (1966), and *Flaming Creatures* (1963), to mention just a few of these filmmakers' most famous works. As the 1970s dawned, lesbian filmmaker Barbara Hammer created a series of compelling short films extolling lesbian desire: *Dyketactics* (1974), *Sisters* (1973), and many others. As with their straight counterparts in the filmic underground, these films acquired a certain currency and notoriety through repeated nonmainstream screenings at museums, festivals, and smaller theaters, and so gradually, over a period of several decades, the heteronormative stranglehold of the production code began to loosen, to be replaced by a more questioning and open cinematic discourse.

As a new generation of actors and directors began making mainstream films, the old proscription that "only Gentiles could be beautiful" (Clarke 133)—as most notably practiced by Louis B. Mayer of MGM (see Clarke 132–33 for details about the "beauty standard" applied by MGM in their films of the 1930s through the 1950s)—was pushed aside. This new generation included actors like Robert De Niro, Harvey Keitel, Christopher Walken, Dustin Hoffman, Barbra Streisand, Sidney Poitier, Dorothy Dandridge, Danny Glover, Wesley Snipes, Samuel L. Jackson, Shirley MacLaine, and Woody Allen, and by directors like Martin Scorsese, Francis Ford Coppola, Jonathan Demme, Kathryn Bigelow, David Cronenberg, Derek Jarman, Stephen Frears, Jim Jarmusch, Todd Haynes, Spike Lee, and Ernest Dickerson. But was this ground shift permanent? Or would these new actors and directors become fixtures in a new white heterocentric cinema, at once more carefully circumscribed and in many ways much more blatant than the dominant imagistic order that had preceded it?

The history of heterosexual display in the cinema is thus a disavowal of the self, a disavowal in which the body functions as a site of
performative management, governed by the economics of consumption. The figurative linkages offered by various heterocentric visions—
family life, children, courtship, sexual desire—are components of a
commercialized discourse that creates a double inversion, forcing the
body back into itself to seek new, less-constricting configurations. The
dreams of investigation epitomized by the mainstream film of heterosexual performativity, as well as by the more direct address of the porn
film, present the viewer with a spectacle of paramnesia, an illusion of
recaptured experience. The discrepancies of action between performative heterosexual display and the stratigraphy of heterosexism itself creates a series of imagistic microfissures, an organization of associations
that is at once redolent of expressive individualism and yet still subject
to the temporal horizons imposed on human social discourse by the
"kinetoscopophiliac" lure of the cinema. As revealed in *The Mummy
Returns,* it is not enough to be a couple—one must also reproduce to
provide proof of the permanence of the heterosexual union. When
there are no children, the family unit is seen as suspect, incomplete:
Are those people *really* heterosexual (that is, "one of us")? Or are they
only pretending to be for the benefit of the audience's entertainment
and reassurance?

In *Leave Her to Heaven* (1945), Ellen Berent (later Harland), the
film's protagonist (played by Gene Tierney), throws herself down a flight
of stairs to induce a miscarriage so that she can have her husband,
Richard Harland (played by Cornel Wilde), all to herself. It is to no avail,
for although her pregnancy is terminated by her actions, so is her marriage. Richard turns to Ellen's cousin, Ruth (Jeanne Crain), for solace
and finds genuine (read *straight*) love. Ellen has also allowed Richard's
brother, Danny (Darryl Hickman), to drown in a lake; again, she wants
no one to compete with her for Richard's affections. Her pathological
behavior is partially explained late in the film's narrative by her mother,
who tells Richard,

> "There's nothing wrong with Ellen . . . it's just that she loves too much . . .
> perhaps that isn't good . . . it makes an outsider of everyone else . . . you
> must be patient with her[;] . . . she loved her father too much." Still later,
> Ellen's cousin Ruth offers a reading of the Berent family system in an angry

FIGURE 17. Jeanne Crain (*left*) and Gene Tierney (*center, with book*) regard each other warily in *Leave Her to Heaven*. Courtesy: Jerry Ohlinger Archives.

flurry aimed at Ellen: "With your love you wrecked mother's life, with your love you pressed father to death, with your love you've made a shadow of Richard." (Renov 233)

Yet what Ellen fears most is the loss of identity that her marriage will bring, a loss of self that matrimony anticipates in the very act of the wedding ceremony itself. Richard and Ellen's marriage is not real, can never be real, because Ellen, a product of postwar American culture, seeks a life for herself above all other considerations and refuses to be subsumed in any relationship. Yet unable to declare her true intentions because of the social conventions of the period, Ellen must lie continually about her relationships, about her actions, and, eventually, even about the manner of her death. As she commits suicide with a lethal dose of poison, Ellen leaves incriminating evidence to frame Ruth for the crime, so that Richard and Ruth will be prevented from marrying (and, the narrative implies, having children).

In *Mildred Pierce* (1945), Joan Crawford's Mildred has a different obsession. For her daughter, Veda (Ann Blyth), she sacrifices her marriage, her restaurant business, and her position within society, until Veda finally overreaches herself with the murder of Monte Beragon (Zachary Scott). Even then, Mildred is willing to shoulder the blame, but she is prevented from doing so through the machinations of the police. Hence Veda, another "feminine monster" of the noir cycle of the 1940s, shuffles off to prison without a shred of remorse.

Despite their differing pathologies, both Ellen Berent and Mildred Pierce are perceived by society as potential sites of racial and social reproduction above all other considerations. They are *women,* and within the strictly defined heterosexually based construct of the cinema couple, womanhood becomes objecthood; simultaneously, womanhood is a responsibility to wed and to bear children, a responsibility to perpetuate the normative heterosexual lifestyle. And inasmuch as both Ellen and Mildred are creations of 1940s Hollywood, and as they are also the putative centers of the narratives they inhabit, they must be white, as are all major figures in American mainstream cinema—and as they have been from the dawn of the studio system to the present day. As Richard Dyer comments,

White women thus carry—or, in many narratives, betray—the hopes, achievements and character of the race. They guarantee its reproduction, even while not succeeding to its highest heights. . . . White women's role in reproduction makes them at once privileged and subordinated in relation to the operation of White power in the world. (*White* 29)

Those who are nonwhite find their options severely limited, even in the lightest of cinematic entertainments, such as transparently contrived escapist musicals. Ella Shohat observes of the film *The Gang's All Here* (1943),

> a generic division of labor, whereby the solid, "serious," or romantic numbers such as "A Journey to a Star" tend to be performed by the North American protagonists Alice Faye and James Ellison, while the Latin American characters perform "unserious," "excessive" numbers involving swaying hips, exaggerated facial expressions, caricaturally sexy costumes, and "think-big" style props embodied by Carmen Miranda[;] . . . exoticizing and eroticizing the Third World allowed the imperial imaginary to play out its own fantasies of sexual domination. (46–47)

Thus is the artificial upheld, the natural suppressed. Gender, after all, is a construct, just as race is, to be imposed or omitted at will. Racial marking is as transient as gender identification; all systems of signification outside the cinema are fluid, no matter how repressive, because either by the tactics of marginalization or by recognized difference, they acknowledge the existence and the mutability of the other. Clothing, makeup, shoes, hats, and other markers of gender within society can be altered at the wearer's will, providing that the system within which that person operates will support it (or will at least allow it) or providing that the person creates a zone of influence that transcends society's normative expectations. Conventional gender constructs support the heterocentric value system because the "disciplinary production of gender effects a false stabilization of gender in the interests of the heterosexual construction and regulation of sexuality within the reproductive domain" (Butler 172). This search for a reified construct was also present during World War II, particularly in the military, where top brass

> informally channeled identifiably gay GIs into a variety of stereotypically homosexual jobs—women became motor vehicle operators and mechanics; men served as clerks, medics, hospital corpsmen, chaplains' assistants, and female impersonators in musical revues and morale-boosting shows. This

tended to create a sense of gay solidarity and community that many GIs—especially those from small towns—had never known before entering the service. (Miller 231)

In short, whatever construct the viewer wishes can be obtained; it's simply a matter of obtaining the right clothing, the right makeup, a dress or a pair of slacks, a man's fedora or a woman's bonnet. And when the usefulness of the masquerade is over, the performer can readily disappear behind the identity he or she has created. As Peggy Phelan comments,

> Performance's only life is in the present. Performance cannot be saved, recorded, documented, or otherwise participate in the circulation of representations *of* representations: once it does so, it becomes something other than performance. To the degree that performance attempts to enter the economy of reproduction it betrays and lessens the promise of its own ontology. Performance's being, like the ontology of subjectivity proposed here, becomes itself through disappearance. (146)

Just as Joan Marshall/Jean Arless vanished at the conclusion of *Homicidal*, so too do we vanish with the usefulness of our performative personae. But Phelan is wrong to say that "[p]erformance cannot be saved, recorded, documented, or otherwise participate in the circulation of representations *of* representations"; this happens all the time. Public faces are adopted, gender roles assigned, makeup and wigs employed to create a construct that is at once evanescent and permanent. As long as the image of this performance remains in our mind's eye, even though not recorded directly, the performance continues to exist, and yet, as Phelan suggests, it has also vanished, as all completed illusions ultimately contain a significatory endgame. Much performance art suggests an extraordinary preoccupation with the prison of flesh that we all inhabit and with the performative sexual roles that we enact each day in order to maintain social contact with those around us (see Schimmel for more details). Consider the performance pieces by Kazuo Shiraga ("Challenging Mud" [1955]), Saburo Murakami ("Breaking through Many Screens of Paper" [1956]), and Atsuko Tanaka ("Electric Press" [1956]), for example, or the "living" paintings of Yves Klein. Klein used nude models as his paintbrushes to create a series of carefully staged media events, at once performative and concrete (as betokened by their remaining artifacts, the paintings themselves). There is also Klein's notorious photomontage "Leap into the

Void" (1960), in which the artist *appears* to fling himself from a window without the benefit of a safety net below. There are other performances as well, including those by Daniel Spoerri, Guiseppe Piriot Gallizio, Allan Kaprow, Ben Vautier, Wolf Vostell, Joseph Beuys, Hermann Nitsch, Yayoi Kusama, Yoko Ono, Otto Muehl, and others.

In many of Nitsch's pieces, which he dubbed "Material Actions," nude women and men were ceremonially wrapped in plastic and wire and then drenched in the intestines of eviscerated animals. This signified the body as a site of inescapable loneliness—each of us cut from the other by the boundaries of flesh, gender, performance, and ritual. The dialogic alterity of such a performative strategy is a clear indication of the dis-ease with which each of us confronts our corporeal isolation, yet the imagistic subjectivism of Nitsch's pieces ensures that each viewer will carry away a different experience from his art, a kind of performative management accomplished by each witness as a discrete unit.

Andy Warhol, arguably more than any other artist in the twentieth century, brought the performative aspect of heterosexuality as a public construct into the public eye. In addition to the torrent of paintings and conventional 16mm films that became his central legacy, Warhol also cre-ated some early experiments with video that center the viewer's gaze upon the act of creation of the self, gay and/or straight. In his 1965 double-screen, double-projector film *Outer and Inner Space,* Warhol used a prim-itive Norelco recorder to videotape Factory starlet Edie Sedgwick; he then played the tapes back on a monitor while Sedgwick sat next to the screen, responding to her videotaped image with a mixture of bemusement and bewilderment. Warhol shot two twelve-hundred-foot reels of 16mm film of Sedgwick confronting her meticulously made-up visage in sync-sound, then he projected them side by side, so that the viewer is shown four close-ups of Edie's face simultaneously; from left to right, video, film, video, film. Which of these images is real? Which is a construct? Are any of these performative heterosexual gazes any more real than another? As Jim Hoberman notes,

> Her lips glossed and eyes shining, a pair of enormous dangling earrings cast-ing a grid of shadows across her graceful neck, the film Sedgwick was never more appealing than here. Poised and elegant, she acts as though it's tea time on Mars. Sedgwick never stops talking, unless it's to draw on her cigarette or pull a face, presumably in response to something she hears her video self

say. The four layers of Sedgwick discourse become a murmuring burble in which only isolated phrases ("We had better times than anybody else," "I don't believe it") float to the surface of audibility. . . . Becoming in a sense her own audience, the "live" Sedgwick often seems startled, distracted, even sometimes distressed by the effect of having her own voice whispering in her ear. ("It makes me so nervous to listen to it," she exclaims at one point.) As its title suggests, *Outer and Inner Space* visualizes a fragmented attention, a schizoid disjunction between public and private selves. (34)

Through the metaphor of film-video translation, the opposition of contradictories present in Sedgwick's performed heterosexual self creates a new antirelativism for the viewer: the production of a gender hybridization that from inclination argues for a complete disavowal of the self in favor of or in deference to the self constructed on the two screens of *Outer and Inner Space*. In her own way, Sedgwick prefigures the denial of the body present in such contemporary icons as Lara Flynn Boyle, Calista Flockhart, Jennifer Aniston, Heather Locklear, and other figures of heterosexual performativity who now dominate public consciousness (just as Sedgwick did in the demimonde of 1960s Manhattan). Television reifies our desire to look like these performers, to act like them, to share their values, so that we may participate in their lives and perhaps become them.

The cinema of the new millennium has also offered viewers the ascendance of the preoperative transgendered or gay cross-dressing sidekick, who shows the straight protagonists of the film how truly to embrace romance in such films as *To Wong Foo, Thanks for Everything, Julie Newmar* (1995), and other, more recent projects. These new-age avatars, unafraid to act out on their desires, express a liberated sexuality that encourages straight audiences to think out of the box, to acknowledge both difference and their own limitations as rigidly defined sexual beings. Ironically, India's "Bollywood" musicals remain one of the last sites of unreconstructed heterosexual romance, as Indian viewers incessantly clamor for the same plot: boy meets girl, boy loses girl, boy gets girl back, with six to ten musical numbers added to sustain viewer interest. Yet this strategy is no longer an option within classic Hollywood cinema.

Heather Addison all too convincingly argues that "the 1990s might be characterized as the decade of romantic decline for family-film musicals" (180).

Clearly, a majority of family films emphasize the importance of social integration, either through romantic coupling or personal maturation. If the films adults make for children are a good marker of their expectations of children, it would seem that adults' main expectation of children is that they become productive, law-abiding citizens who do not disturb the status quo. (189)

Musicals, along with westerns, have achieved the onanistic intention of pornography; through their endlessly repetitive organization of associations, their components of discourse have become exhausted. There is little to repeat or even to recreate. Attaining the pure virtuality of constructed social guidance tracts, the inherent and transparently obvious artificiality of motion picture musicals has assured their domestic demise.

In *What Women Want* (2000), Mel Gibson becomes more sympathetic—both to the narrow configuration of his own sexual being and to the needs of heterosexual women—as a result of a freak accident that allows him to hear the thoughts of straight women who objectify and/or appraise his heteroperformative sexual presence on a daily basis. In *Tootsie* (1982), Dustin Hoffman learns to embrace a kinder, gentler heterosexism as a result of spending time in drag. Robin Williams undergoes a similar transformation in *Mrs. Doubtfire* (1993). His character learns the responsibilities that come with the heterosexual lifestyle (a wife, children, a house with a mortgage), after dressing up as a British nanny to infiltrate his former household (his wife banished him as a consequence of his incorrigible unreliability). Predictably, a character played by Harvey Fierstein is on hand to give Williams's character makeup tips, as well as to counsel him on the way to reaffirm himself as the man of the house.

Talk, performance, action, rehearsal, presentation, but little actual sex; in the age of AIDS, people talk about sex, but they abstain from it. In *sex, lies and videotape* (1989), the character played by James Spader, unable or unwilling to engage in actual sexual contact, videotapes the oral histories of his various subjects' sex lives. For those with the inclination, cybersex and phone sex offer a distancing from risk and a certain amount of satisfaction. In an age when a president's sex life becomes fair game not just for the tabloids but for the traditional press as well, cybercoupling seems both safer and more convenient.

As the family unit in real life crumbles, with more single mothers and absent fathers in recent years than at any time in recent memory, viewers

feel the need to create a new extended family of friends and acquain-
tances: street gangs offer runaways and other teens a synthetic sense of
belonging; for many Americans, the characters on *Friends, Dawson's
Creek, Party of Five,* and an array of daytime and nighttime soaps have
become imaginary relatives, the roommates and people you never knew,
whose lives occupy a zone of endless leisure, health, and carefully dia-
grammed heteroperformative display. *Scream and Scream Again* (1970)
posits the existence of a race of synthetically created androids who are so
perfect that they pass for human within the confines of everyday society;
Looker (1981) predicts the creation of male and female heterosexual
cybermodels to sell products and promote political aspirants on television, almost exactly the same strategy that is being pursued by advertisers
today. Cars, clothing, even food products are heterosexualized. "Eat me!"
commands a manic, live-action, masculine heteroperformative Slim Jim
in commercials for the ubiquitous snack food. The commercial and sexual message is clear: when we eat Slim Jims, we eat ourselves.

The rise of public interest in *animé,* the Japanese semirealistic, hypersexualized, ceaselessly violent adult cartoons, is also a reflection of our
search for an idealized self-image. Like the waxen, robotic humanoids on
display in *Shrek* (2001)—figures that are much less convincing than the
rotoscoped Snow White in *Snow White and the Seven Dwarfs* (1937)—
these humanoid simulacra have all the attributes of human existence
except humanity. And as American culture becomes more isolationist,
with foreign films routinely being remade in English rather than being
released in their original languages with subtitles (it's *so* difficult to watch
and read at the same time, they imply)—thus stripping the films not only
of their cultural currency, but also of their performers, costumes, sets, and
sense of contradictoriness through the metaphor of translation—only
those films that mark a return to "Orientalism," such as *Crouching Tiger,
Hidden Dragon* (2000), still attract audiences. Subtitles here remain
"appropriate"; after all, isn't this a *foreign* film?

The multivoiced address of cinema in the early 1900s, when all films
were silent and required only new intertitles to translate their images for
various audiences, and the prevideo domain of subtitled or dubbed foreign films competing on an even basis with American films (*Psycho* meets
La Dolce vita [both 1960] at your local theater) has been abandoned. Even
dubbing is unacceptable, except in Jackie Chan action films, where the
asynchronous lip matching of the characters' speaking that Geoffrey

O'Brien has aptly called "post-synchronese" seems to add to the sense of cultural displacement (164). We require all othered experiences to be translated to our own cultural milieu, or we are seemingly not interested in them at all. For in such films as *Crouching Tiger, Hidden Dragon,* and in the Jackie Chan, Jean-Claude Van Damme, Bruce Lee, and Jet Li non-stop-action films, action has replaced romance as the social currency on display. The recent wave of interest in Hong Kong action films foreshadows a culture in which violence replaces thought, endless aggression replaces dialogue, and the warrior-opponent model does away with the structured conceit of the two heterosexual lovers, locked together in eternal embrace.

In contemporary cinema, men are seen in straight relationships as being necessary accouterments rather than partners, as evinced in the title of the recent film *Boys on the Side* (1995). This film and many others, such as *Waiting to Exhale* (1995), *The First Wives Club* (1996), and *How Stella Got Her Groove Back* (1998), may be seen as a series of feminist correctives to such films as *She Had to Say Yes* (1933), *Shopworn* (1932), and *Kind Lady* (1936, 1951), in which women were perpetually dependent upon the men in their lives. Similarly, when lesbianism and homosexuality first appeared as the central subject matter of mainstream films in the 1960s, the narrative conclusions of such films as *The Killing of Sister George* (1968) and *The Boys in the Band* (1970) were predictably downbeat. As late as 1994, with *Heavenly Creatures,* intimate same-sex attachments were seen as unhealthy, and as a threat to the stability of 1950s New Zealand family life (which, in this case, it indeed was). In our contemporary visions of the past, we view what once seemed a heterotopia as a dysfunctional performance of bondage, in sitcoms like *That '70s Show,* where an autocratic, mean-spirited husband wields dimwitted authority over his compliant, obviously unhappy partner.

The British and American versions of *Queer as Folk* (but especially the British version), offer a new utopia for lesbians and gays, a world in which (most of) society is tolerant; mothers and fathers eventually prove understanding after initial bewilderment; and—as in *Friends*—no one really has to work and can thus feel free to party all night long. The 1950s bedchamber has been replaced by the new millennium's bondage chamber, as *Queer as Folk* seeks to titillate while concomitantly using societal acceptance of the series as a barometer of public opinion. The famously dysfunctional, straight, Italian Catholic Soprano household lurches from disaster to disaster week after week on *The Sopranos,* just as J. R. Ewing and his clan did in the long-running teleseries *Dallas,* but to what avail? The straight home has become a battleground in which all participants, male and female, children and adults, continually strive to manipulate matters to gain even momentary advantage. *Law and Order,* now spun off into the original and two companion series, presents us with an unending succession of unfaithful husbands, murderous wives, homicidal children, corrupt businessmen, incompetent judges, burned-out social workers—a landscape of complete desolation and hopelessness. The perpetrator of this week's offense may be caught, may be guilty and brought to trial, and may even receive a sentence commensurate with his or her misdeeds. But the victory is illusory; tomorrow will bring more transgression, more violence, and further evidence of social decay. *Family Law* deals solely with the spectacle of the straight family unit in freefall, as does *Judging Amy;* both shows are filled with incessant, desperate pleas for men and women to assume the duties of parenthood they have obviously neglected. Single mothers and/or fathers are seen as suspect; surely, the child in question would fare better in a two-parent household, the last bastion of performative social management. At the same time, a proliferation of real-life high-profile adoptions fills the tabloids with sentimental instant-family warmth—though many of the celebrities adopting children eventually divorce and their adoptive offspring are left at the center of a bitter battle for custody, visitation rights, and/or material property (assuming the child had been adopted into a two-parent home in the first place). All of this takes place against the backdrop of the actual destruction of welfare as a social system in the United States. Poor single mothers must now work at whatever menial job they can in order to pay for rent, food, and clothing; the jobs often pay less than seven dollars an hour, forcing them to work multiple shifts or two or more jobs. But for the rich, the new patricians of wealth and power, the heterocentric dream of the male remains the Stepford Wife, eternally perfect and utterly docile; while heterosexual women seek men with power, status, and money to furnish their domestic domain. Clothing—rather than one's interior world—is now the signifier of a person's worth; on the E! cable network, Melissa and Joan Rivers discuss the various borrowed gowns that celebrities wear to the Academy Awards, the Tonys, the Grammys, and other awards shows—accomplishment is nothing, appearance is all.

And what happens when one has "consumed" one's self, given to the publicity machines all that one has, and outlived one's social usefulness as a cinematic icon? Nineteen sixties star Capucine started her Hollywood career with such major films as *North to Alaska* (1960), *The Pink Panther* (1964), and *What's New, Pussycat?* (1965), but as the decade wound down, Capucine found that her star currency was no longer in demand. Retreating to her native Europe, she was lured out of forced retirement for *Arabian Adventure* (1979), *Trail of the Pink Panther* (1982), and *Curse of the Pink Panther* (1983), before retreating entirely to her apartment in Lausanne, Switzerland. Her last two films, which were also the last two entries in the *Pink Panther* series, were filmed simultaneously so that director Blake Edwards could assemble his original cast, including Peter Sellers (in footage shot for earlier installments of the series, in addition to unused scenes and outtakes; Sellers had died in 1980), David Niven (*Curse* was Niven's final film, and his rapidly failing health made it necessary for impressionist Rich Little to dub Niven's voice), Herbert Lom, Robert Wagner, and of course, Capucine. But Blake Edwards's pastiche failed to reignite the public's interest in the still-chic star. By 1990, Capucine was crippled by depression, and she jumped to her death from the terrace of her eighth-floor apartment. She had lived for the public, for the public's acceptance and approbation, and when this was denied her, she saw no reason to continue her existence. In this light, in the straight cinema's unceasing appetite for the new and disregard for the old, it is that cruelest of institutions, a sacrificial altar upon which one depends for all external validation.

We have now come to a time when the position of the director as auteur has never been weaker in Hollywood; it is now the producers who have the power. As late as the 1970s and 1980s, directors within the studio system were able to operate with some degree of autonomy and see their vision survive relatively intact on the theater screen; then, runaway budgets and the advent of video made the "smaller" film almost obsolete, although occasional sleeper hits still break through. Most noticeable in the new regime, however, is a lack of individual vision; the new movies are a product of the conglomerates that create them, and nothing more. As Peter Bart accurately observes, the new "McMovie" is an altogether different entertainment experience.

The impact of this seismic shift is now drastically evident at the multiplex. The film fare of the moment is uniquely risk averse; lots of movies have roman numerals after their titles, because sequels are safer, albeit more expensive, to produce. . . .

. . . In PlayStation cinema, scenes become data chunks as dialogue gives way to algorithms. Conventional screenplay structures are banished. Time no longer moves in a straight line. There's no need for the classic three-act screenplay structure when one crazed montage of hyperkinetic data chunks will do. ("State" 210)

The media conglomerates are also intent on denying viewers access to an alternative system of images, one that might make them question the new McMovies they're forced to consume. Hollywood controls the world's box office, and it is Hollywood products that filmgoers around the globe flock to see, neglecting their own culture and its artifacts with seldom a backward glance. Cultural critic Christopher Hitchens, in an interview with Cynthia Cotts, argues that while "we live in a culture where globalization is a mantra, many media companies are cutting down on foreign coverage" (qtd. in Cotts 30). Cotts notes, "By doing so, [Hitchens] suggests, we risk lapsing into a mind-set prevalent in the Middle Ages, when maps of the world dubbed unknown parts to be *in partibus infidelium,* or in the land of the infidel" (30).

In France, director François Ozon has established a reputation for dystopian visions of the heterocentric unit, beginning with his breakthrough featurette, *See the Sea* (1998). The cultural difference is important here, for Ozon is one of the new generation of filmmakers—one who has grown up in the age of video games and fragmented editing styles—and yet he has resisted the drift toward cyclonic blenderization of images in his own work, which is at once sinister and measured, recalling the minimal insistence of Robert Bresson or Jean-Marie Straub. In *See the Sea,* a young woman named Sasha (played by Sasha Hails) is left alone in her bourgeois home with her baby when her husband leaves on a business trip. Almost immediately, a sullen young woman, Tatiana (Marina de Van), appears at the front door, demanding permission to camp on the front lawn. Sasha is rightly suspicious of Tatiana's true intentions, but she is also lonely, and so she permits the woman to pitch her tent in the front yard. Gradually, Tatiana becomes more and more attached to Sasha's baby, and Sasha, seemingly overwhelmed by the duties of motherhood, is more than willing to accept Tatiana's assistance. It is a fatal mistake. When Sasha's husband returns home, he discovers Sasha's body, bound and mutilated, inside the

FIGURE 18. Sasha Hails *(left)* and Marina de Van in François Ozon's *See the Sea.* Courtesy: Jerry Ohlinger Archives.

tent Tatiana had erected. Their child is gone. Ozon cuts to a final sequence of Tatiana holding the infant on a boat. The baby seems quite content, utterly unaware of what has transpired; its new mother has replaced Sasha, and no one will ever know the difference. It is unlikely, Ozon suggests, that Tatiana will ever be brought to justice for her crime. Ozon stages all of this with a calm deliberation worthy of Yasujiro Ozu or Carl Theodor Dreyer; one shot replaces another with authority and assurance. As with Claire Denis's *Beau travail* (1998), the camera is never in a hurry; it absorbs the atmosphere of the desolate island where the action of *See the Sea* transpires, unhurried, contemplative. The audience is left to interpret the images being presented without overt manipulations, whether through editorial structure, the arc of the film's narrative, or intrusive music cues. Ozon notes:

> In order to follow the development of the two characters, the film was shot in chronological order. I was somewhat unsure, in a haze, about certain scenes, but building on what we had shot, things became more obvious as we went along.
>
> Besides, we had to follow the life patterns of the baby and to respect her hours of sleep. We used no tricks to make her cry; she would naturally do so as soon as her mother left her sight.
>
> I didn't want Sasha to know the story. I wanted her to be virgin to the plot and discover it day by day. I just told her it was about herself and her baby, and that it was set on an island. I believe that this way of shooting left her free, so she could act without anticipating too much.
>
> Points of view were the true problem of the directing: When to quit Sasha's point of view to enter Tatiana's? I finally decided that the film would be shot almost exclusively from Sasha's point of view, with scraps of Tatiana's contaminating the story here and there. I shot the scenes seen through Tatiana's eyes (at the supermarket and in the graveyard) without knowing where they would go. I only found their place during the editing. The feeling of danger pervading the realistic and everyday-like scenes of Sasha comes from the insertion of those scenes. I wished to show blocks of time without giving any explanations or psychological justifications. I just wanted to impart sensations, impressions and signs that the audience would be free to accept or reject. Journeys are shot in real time whereas they are normally shortened. I wanted the audience to have time to ask itself questions from which anxiety and suspense would derive.

Just as Ozon's film depicts the straight nuclear family unit as fragile, in need of constant maintenance, and ultimately a fiction, Thomas Vinterberg's digital film *Celebration* (1998) documents the ruinous reunion of a family haunted by the ghost of child abuse. The father in *Celebration* is revealed to be a pederast who, protected by the straight family code of silence, has been raping his children for years. At this particular gathering, the children, now grown up, force even his wife to accept the father's decades of abuse and exile him from the family circle. The father's forced exit, after a weekend of drunken revels and midnight confessions, is the film's triumphant resolution, but the victory is one of utter faithlessness—the endangered family unit has collapsed under the weight of its own pretense.

Perhaps it would be well to let the stars themselves have the last word on the commodification of desire represented by the pluralistic decentralization of the expressive presentation of performative heterosexuality in the Hollywood cinema. Actors, no longer individuals, have become public property, mere ghosts of themselves for public representation. And in no sense are they in real life what they appear to be on the screen. They forfeit their privacy and, to a degree, their human identity. Kevin Costner commented in 1996, "A lot of doors have been closed to me because of fame and celebrity, but an equal amount of doors opened. If you ask about trading things for anonymity, if I would go back, the answer is an absolute yes" (qtd. in Berlin 193). While Luke Perry said,

> It dawned on me that people would notice when I went somewhere, but you can't let that hold you back. I'm not going to become a prisoner of what I think is a great situation, the fact that I've been afforded the opportunity to work as an actor. I'm not going to turn around and let that control me. And you know what? I have a lot of friends who are famous now, who were famous at one time, or who will certainly be famous in the future. Actors here in Hollywood, we know who's into being famous and who's into getting work. I would much rather continue to be a working actor than a famous one. The fame is a by-product of the work. (qtd. in Berlin 196–97)

And, perhaps not surprisingly, Paul Newman cut closest to the mark when he observed of cinema audiences,

> They really think that that's me up there. That isn't me. It's somebody else, somebody some writer concocted and some actor dragged together and some director splashed up there. The director edited all the bad moments out and left the good moments and they think that's real up there. It really isn't. It has nothing to do with me. (qtd. in Berlin 204)

But if Paul Newman's iconic image as a film actor isn't him, then who or what is it? Angelina Jolie isn't really Dr. Lara Croft in *Tomb Raider* (2001); she's a construct based on a video game, which appeals primarily to bored adolescents. She's also Jon Voight's daughter, who plays her father in the film, adding another layer of self-reflexivity to the project. Heath Ledger in *A Knight's Tale* (2001) is no more real than Bing Crosby was in *A Connecticut Yankee in King Arthur's Court* (1949), and both characters owe their existence, no matter how ephemeral, to the imagination of a nearly bankrupt Mark Twain, who had been looking for a new story to pay off old debts (and who, as everyone knows, wasn't really Mark Twain at all). Jennifer Lopez's *Angel Eyes* (2001) stare at the viewer from the film's poster with soft intensity, as the rest of her facial features vanish in an evanescent haze reminiscent of *Eyes without a Face* (1959). Haley Joel Osment really *isn't* real in *A.I. Artificial Intelligence* (2001), the tale of an adorable, white, male adolescent who is actually an android (a project begun by Stanley Kubrick, that most detached of directors, and then shepherded to the screen by Steven Spielberg, that most manipulative of filmmakers, after Kubrick's death). Hugh Jackman in *Swordfish* (2001) plays an ace computer hacker possessed of code-breaking skills capable of bringing down an entire corporation, working with John Travolta, Don Cheadle, and a nearly nude Halle Berry. Freddie Prinze, Jr., and Jessica Biel ask, "Are you game?" in *Summer Catch* (2001), a heterocentric sports film that presents the baseball diamond as the ideal location for heteroperformative bonding. Nicole Kidman and Ewan McGregor fall in love in *Moulin Rouge* (2001), a curious blend of anachronistic pop songs and Busby Berkeleyesque excess. Sylvester Stallone, Burt Reynolds, Kip Pardue, Til Schweiger, Gina Gershon, and Estella Warren are all driven to win at any cost in the synthetically dangerous world of cinema car racing in *Driven* (2001), where all the crashes and excitement are as artificially generated as the relationships between the characters. Renée Zellweger, Colin Firth, and Hugh Grant are trapped in the pages—and thus the frames—of *Bridget Jones's Diary* (2001); while Woody Allen, Dan Aykroyd, Helen Hunt, and Charlize Theron must contend with *The Curse of the Jade Scorpion* (2001). *Dr. Dolittle 2* (2001) still talks to the animals; *Crocodile Dundee in Los Angeles* (2001) is quite at home; and Nicolas Cage and Penélope Cruz inhabit a reconstructed World War II romance in *Captain Corelli's Mandolin* (2001). It's all business as usual.

What sold yesterday will sell today, and what sells today will continue to attract audiences tomorrow. Straightness *sells*.

If heterosexuality has any currency at all at the dawn of the twenty-first century, it is as an artifact demanding constant rejuvenation and reification in much the same way that the Mummy (in all his screen appearances, from 1932 onward) is in danger of disintegration unless he receives constant maintenance. The labels stick, and if they fall off, they do damage; this we know. The public's fear of the other, reinforced by decades of cinemagoing, is never more in evidence than in the present social climate, in which the politics of repression and denial have become the national currency.

If the movies of the twenty-first century seek to teach us anything, it is that we will never be satisfied; we will never truly come to any fixed point of social or sexual fixed ground. We will always want more, and more again, but we will never be truly satiated. It is our lot to continually seek the phantom reassurance of a new imagistic construct that can never fulfill our spectatorial desires. Viewers of twenty-first-century cinema are consumers first and audiences second; the product must never satisfy, so that we will return for another fix. Lost in a wilderness of conflicting images, moving ever faster, with quicker and quicker editing until the unit of the cinema shot itself collapses, we are finally stripped of any fugitive identity we may have thought we possessed. Where will we go when we discover that we no longer exist? What will we do when the illusion, finally unable to bear the weight of its own construction, collapses in a double inversion of its figurative linkages?

The disavowal of the self that the construction of being straight represents cannot survive without the continual production of images to support it, work that is going on now with a renewed, desperate intensity because the economic and social stakes are so much higher. What will replace the discrepancies of action that constitute straight discourse in contemporary cinema? For the moment, it seems that we are destined ceaselessly to repeat the past, hoping to find there some semblance of security and safety. The alternative seems too terrible to contemplate. What will we do when we are forced, at last, to see ourselves?

WORKS CITED
AND CONSULTED

Acker, Ally. *Real Women: Pioneers of the Cinema.* New York: Continuum, 1991.

Acker, Kathy. "The End of the World of White Men." *Posthuman Bodies.* Ed. Judith Halberstam and Ira Livingston. Bloomington: Indiana UP, 1995. 57–72.

Addison, Heather. "Children's Films in the 1990s." *Film Genre 2000.* Ed. Wheeler Winston Dixon. Albany: State U of New York P, 2000. 177–91.

"AMC Says It Will Close Up to 20% of Its Movie Screens." *New York Times* 26 Jan. 2001: C3.

American Civil Liberties Union. "House Vote on Same Sex Marriage: H.R. 3396." 25 July 2001 <http://www.aclu.org/vote-guide/House_HR3396.html>.

Anders, Allison. "Glean Living: Agnès Varda on Life, Filmmaking and *The Gleaners and I.*" *Res* 4.3 (2001): 34–35.

Anger, Kenneth. *Hollywood Babylon.* San Francisco: Straight Arrow, 1975.

———. *Hollywood Babylon II.* New York: Dutton, 1984.

Arce, Hector. *The Secret Life of Tyrone Power.* New York: Morrow, 1979.

Arthurs, Jane. "*Thelma and Louise:* On the Road to Feminism?" *Feminist Subject, Multi-Media, Cultural Methodologies.* Ed. Penny Florence and Dee Reynolds. Manchester, UK: Manchester UP, 1995. 89–105.

Baard, Erik. "The DNA Bomb." *Village Voice* 22 May 2001: 34–40.

Babbit, Jamie. Personal interview. 21 Oct. 2000.

Bailey, F. G. *The Prevalence of Deceit.* Ithaca, NY: Cornell UP, 1991.

Barr, Charles. *Ealing Studios.* London: Cameron/David, 1977.

Barson, Michael, and Steven Heller. *Red Scared!: The Commie Menace in Propaganda and Popular Culture.* San Francisco: Chronicle, 2001.

Bart, Peter. "The *Other* Arnold." *GQ* Oct. 1995: 89+.

———. "State of the Art." *GQ* Dec. 2000: 208+.

Bates, James. "Actors, Ad Firms Reach Tentative Deal to End Strike." *Los Angeles Times* 23 Oct. 2000: A1+.

Baudrillard, Jean. *The Illusion of the End.* Trans. Chris Turner. Stanford: Stanford UP, 1994.

Behlmer, Rudy, ed. *Memo from David O. Selznick.* New York: Viking, 1972.

Bergan, Ronald. *The United Artists Story.* New York: Crown, 1986.

Berlin, Joey. *Toxic Fame: Celebrities Speak on Stardom.* Detroit: Visible Ink, 1996.

Berube, Allan, and John D'Emilio. *Coming Out under Fire: The History of Gay Men and Women in World War II.* Chicago: U of Chicago P, 1985.

Bhabha, Homi K. *The Location of Culture.* New York: Routledge, 1994.

Binkin, Martin, and Shirley T. Bach. *Women and the Military.* Washington, DC: Brookings Institute, 1977.

Birchall, Danny. "Thieves Like Us." *Sight and Sound* Oct. 2000: 32+.

———. "Yellow Brick Code: Jack Valenti Fights Hollywood's Corner against DVD Piracy." *Sight and Sound* Oct. 2000: 35.

Blair, Frederika. *Isadora.* Wellingborough, UK: Equation, 1987.

Borow, Zev. "Advances in Advertising: Corporate Bigwigs Go Undercover in the Name of Cool." *New Yorker* 23–30 Aug. 1999: 58+.

Bosworth, Patricia. *Montgomery Clift: A Biography.* New York: Harcourt, 1978.

Bourdon, David. *Warhol.* New York: Abrams, 1989.

Bright, Morris, and Robert Ross. Carry On *Uncensored.* London: Boxtree, 1999.

Brownlow, Kevin. *The Parade's Gone By.* New York: Knopf, 1968.

Butler, Judith. *Gender Trouble: Feminism and the Subversion of Identity.* New York: Routledge, 1999.

Cagin, Seth, and Philip Dray. *Born to Be Wild: Hollywood and the Sixties Generation.* Boca Raton, FL: Coyote, 1994.

Calder, Jenni. *There Must Be a Lone Ranger.* London: Hamilton, 1974.

Califia, Pat. *Sapphistry: The Book of Lesbian Sexuality.* Tallahassee: Naiad, 1988.

Canemaker, John. *Tex Avery: The MGM Years, 1942–1955.* North Dighton, MA: JG, 1998.

Cannom, Robert C. *Van Dyke and the Mythical City Hollywood.* Culver City, CA: Murray, 1948.

Carson, Tom. "Groping for Something Inspirational in a Sneak Attack." *New York Times* 20 May 2001, sec. 2: 21+.

Case, Sue Ellen, Philip Brett, and Susan Leigh Foster. *Cruising the Performative: Interventions into the Representation of Ethnicity, Nationality, and Sexuality.* Bloomington: Indiana UP, 1995.

Cawthorne, Nigel. *Sex Lives of the Hollywood Idols.* London: Prion, 1997.

Ceplar, Larry, and Steven Englund. *The Inquisition in Hollywood.* Garden City, NY: Anchor/Doubleday, 1980.

Ceram, C. W. *Archaeology of the Cinema.* Trans. Richard Winston. New York: Harcourt, 1965.

Clark, Danae. *Negotiating Hollywood: The Cultural Politics of Actors' Labor.* Minneapolis: U of Minnesota P, 1995.

Clark, David B. *The Cinematic City.* London: Routledge, 1997.

Clarke, Gerald. *Get Happy: The Life of Judy Garland.* New York: Delta, 2000.

Coffee, Lenore. *Storyline.* London: Cassell, 1973.

Cohan, Steven, and Ina Rae Hark. *Screening the Male: Exploring Masculinities in Hollywood Cinema.* London: Routledge, 1993.

Coker, Cheo Hodari. "Brave New Worlds." *Premiere* May 1999: 78–89.

Cornell, Katharine. *I Wanted to Be an Actress.* New York: Random, 1938.

Cotts, Cynthia. "Hitchens Goes Global: Covering the Land of the Infidel." *Village Voice* 22 May 2001: 30.

Crisp, Quentin. *Manners from Heaven: A Divine Guide to Good Behavior.* New York: Harper, 1984.

Curtis, David, ed. *A Directory of British Film and Video Artists.* Luton, UK: Libbey, 1996.

Dardis, Tom. *Some Time in the Sun.* New York: Scribner's, 1986.

Daum, Raymond. *Walking with Garbo: Conversations and Recollections.* New York: HarperCollins, 1991.

Davies, Russell. Introduction. *The Kenneth Williams Diaries.* By Kenneth Williams. Ed. Russell Davies. London: HarperCollins, 1993. xi–xxix.

——— . Introduction. *The Kenneth Williams Letters.* By Kenneth Williams. Ed. Russell Davies. London: HarperCollins, 1994. xi–xvii.

De Acosta, Mercedes. *Here Lies the Heart.* New York: Reynal, 1960.

Debord, Guy. *The Society of the Spectacle.* Trans. Donald Nicholson-Smith. New York: Zone, 1995.

"'Defense of Marriage Act' 5/96 H.R. 3396 Summary/Analysis." 'Lectric Law Library. 25 July 2001 <http://www.lectlaw.com/files/leg23.htm>.

Deivert, Bert. "Shots in Cyberspace: Film Research on the Internet." *Cinema Journal* 35.1 (Fall 1995): 103–24.

Dekkers, Midas. *The Way of All Flesh: The Romance of Ruins.* Trans. Sherry Marx-Macdonald. New York: Farrar, 2000.

de la Colina, José, and Tomás Pérez Turrent. *Objects of Desire: Conversations with Luis Buñuel.* Trans. and ed. Paul Lenti. New York: Marsilio, 1992.

De Man, Paul. *The Resistance to Theory.* Minneapolis: U of Minnesota P, 1986.

Diawara, Manthia. *African Cinema: Politics and Culture.* Bloomington: Indiana UP, 1992.

DiBattista, Maria. *Fast-Talking Dames.* New Haven: Yale UP, 2001.

Dick, Bernard F. *City of Dreams: The Making and Remaking of Universal Pictures.* Lexington: UP of Kentucky, 1997.

Dixon, Wheeler Winston. *The Exploding Eye: A Re-Visionary History of 1960s American Experimental Cinema.* Albany: State U of New York P, 1997.

Doane, Mary Ann. *Femmes Fatales: Feminism, Film Theory, and Psychoanalysis.* New York: Routledge, 1991.

Doherty, Thomas. *Pre-Code Hollywood: Sex, Immorality, and Insurrection in the American Cinema 1930–1934.* New York: Columbia UP, 1999.

————. *Teenagers and Teenpics: The Juvenilization of American Movies in the 1950s.* Boston: Hyman, 1988.

Dolan, Deirdre. "Shoptalk: The Art of the Pitch." *New York Times Magazine* 12 Nov. 2000: 54+.

Donati, William. *Ida Lupino: A Biography.* Lexington: UP of Kentucky, 1996.

Doty, Alexander. *Making Things Perfectly Queer: Interpreting Mass Culture.* Minneapolis: U of Minnesota P, 1993.

Downey, Robert, Sr. Telephone interview. 3 Mar. 2001.

Doyle, Jennifer, Jonathan Flatley, and José Estaban Muñoz. *Pop Out: Queer Warhol.* Durham: Duke UP, 1996.

Duncan, Jody. "Quick Cuts: Maximum *Speed.*" *Cinefex* 59 (Sept. 1994): 89–92.

Dyer, Richard. *Stars.* New ed. London: BFI, 1998.

————. *White.* London: Routledge, 1997.

Eastaugh, Kenneth. *The* Carry On *Book.* London: David, 1978.

Edmondson, Adrian. Web site. 6 June 2001 <http://www.michael.phatcatz.net/ awtv/Comedy/Edmondson/Edmondson.htm1> and <http://www.geocities. com/TelevisionCity/Satellite/2103/index.html>.

Ehrenstein, David. *Open Secret: Gay Hollywood 1928–2000.* New York: Perennial/HarperCollins, 2000.

Ehrlich, Linda C., and David Desser, eds. *Cinematic Landscapes: Observations on the Visual Arts and Cinema and Japan.* Austin: U of Texas P, 1994.

Eisler, Benita. *Class Act: America's Last Dirty Secret.* New York: Watts, 1977.

Elley, Derek. Review of *Guest House Paradiso. Variety* 20 Dec. 1999: 59.

Esquire, with Scotty Welch, eds. *Esquire's Handbook for Hosts.* New York: Grosset, 1953.

————. *What Every Young Man Should Know.* New York: Random, 1962.

Faderman, Lillian. *Odd Girls and Twilight Lovers: A History of Lesbian Life in Twentieth Century America.* New York: Columbia UP, 1991.

Fagan, Herb. *White Hats and Silver Spurs: Interviews with 24 Stars of Film and Television Westerns of the Thirties throughout the Sixties.* Jefferson, NC: McFarland, 1996.

Fenin, George N., and William K. Everson. *The Western: From Silents to Cinerama*. New York: Orion, 1963.

Figgis, Mike, ed. *Projections 10: Hollywood Film-Makers on Film-Making*. London: Faber, 1999.

Finestein, Beth A., ed. *Bisexuality: The Psychology and Politics of an Invisible Minority*. Thousand Oaks, CA: Sage, 1996.

Flagman, Roland. *Thalberg: The Last Tycoon with the World of MGM*. New York: Crown, 1994.

Florence, Penny, and Dee Reynolds, eds. *Feminist Subjects, Multi-Media, Cultural Methodologies*. Manchester, UK: Manchester UP, 1995.

Fontana, Benedetto. *Hegemony and Power: On the Relation between Gramsci and Machiavelli*. Minneapolis: U of Minnesota P, 1993.

Foster, Gwendolyn Audrey. *Captive Bodies: Postcolonial Subjectivity in Cinema*. Albany: State U of New York P, 1999.

———. *Women Film Directors: An International Bio-Critical Dictionary*. Westport, CT: Greenwood, 1995.

Foucault, Michel. *Discipline and Punish: The Birth of the Prison*. Trans. Alan Sheridan. New York: Vintage, 1979.

———. *An Introduction*. Vol. 1 of *The History of Sexuality*. Trans. Robert Hurley. New York: Random, 1990.

———. *The Care of the Self*. Vol. 3 of *The History of Sexuality*. Trans. Robert Hurley. New York: Pantheon, 1986.

Fraser, George MacDonald. *The Hollywood History of the World: From* One Million Years B.C. *to* Apocalypse Now. New York: Fawcett, 1988.

Frayling, Christopher. *Spaghetti Westerns: Cowboys and Europeans from Karl May to Sergio Leone*. London: Tauris, 1998.

French, Peter A. *Cowboy Metaphysics: Ethics and Death in Westerns*. Lanham, MD: Rowman, 1997.

Frow, John. *Cultural Studies and Cultural Value*. Oxford: Clarendon, 1995.

Fury, David. *Johnny Weissmuller: Twice the Hero*. Minneapolis: Artist's, 2000.

Gallico, Paul. "Polyandry for All." *What Every Young Man Should Know*. Ed. *Esquire,* with Scotty Welch. New York: Random, 1962. 219–29.

Garber, Marjorie. *Bisexuality and the Eroticism of Everyday Life*. New York: Routledge, 2000.

Gardner, Gordon. *The Censorship Papers: Movie Censorship Letters from the Hays Office, 1934–1968*. New York: Dodd, 1987.

"Georges Méliès." Missing Link. 25 July 2001 *<http://www.kjenkins49.fsnet.co. uk/index.htm>*.

Germain, David. " *'Harbor'* Tweaked for Japan, Germany." Associated Press Dispatch. 22 May 2001. 8 June 2001. <news.excite.ca/news/ap/010522/18/ pearl-harbor-changes2>.

Gilbert, Elizabeth. "My Favorite Martian." *GQ* Mar. 2001: 331–35.

Giroux, Henry A. *Disturbing Pleasures: Learning Popular Culture*. New York: Routledge, 1994.

Gledhill, Christine, ed. *Home Is Where the Heart Is: Studies in Melodrama and the Woman's Film*. London: BFI, 1987.

Glynn, Kevin. *Tabloid Culture: Trash Taste, Popular Power, and the Transformation of American Television*. Durham: Duke UP, 2000.

Goodwin, Cliff. *Sid James*. London: Century, 1995.

Gordon, Suzanne. *Prisoners of Men's Dreams*. Boston: Little, 1991.

Gray, Beverly. *Roger Corman: The Unauthorized Biography of the Godfather of Indie Filmmaking*. Los Angeles: Renaissance, 2000.

Griffith, Richard, and Arthur Mayer. *The Movies: The Sixty-Year Story of the World of Hollywood and Its Effect on America, from Pre-Nickelodeon Days to the Present*. New York: Bonanza, 1957.

Grover, Ronald, and Stefani Eads. "Hollyweb Flops." *Business Week e.biz* 23 Oct. 2000: EB 124–26+.

Guffey, Robert. "Comic Book Conspiracy." *Steamshovel Press* 17 (2001): 24–28.

Hadleigh, Boze. *Conversations with My Elders*. New York: St. Martin's, 1986.

———. *Hollywood Babble On*. New York: Birch, 1994.

———. *Hollywood Gays*. New York: Barricade, 1996.

———. *Hollywood Lesbians*. New York: Barricade, 1994.

———. *The Lavender Screen: The Gay and Lesbian Films: Their Stars, Makers, Characters, and Critics*. New York: Citadel, 1993.

Halberstam, Judith, and Ira Livingston, eds. *Posthuman Bodies.* Bloomington: Indiana UP, 1995.

Hall, Mordaunt. "Gold and Cocktails." *New York Times* 11 Dec. 1922: 22.

Hall, Stephen S. "The Bully in the Mirror." *New York Times Magazine* 22 Aug. 1999: 30–35+.

Hansen, Arlen J. *Expatriate Paris: A Cultural and Literary Guide to Paris of the 1920s.* New York: Arcade, 1990.

Haun, Harry. *The Cinematic Century: An Intimate Diary of America's Affair with the Movies.* New York: Applause, 2000.

Head, Edith, and Paddy Calistro. *Edith Head's Hollywood.* New York: Dutton, 1983.

Heller, Scott. "Scholars Contemplate the Future of Film Studies in a World of Fast-Changing Technology." *Chronicle of Higher Education* 27 Oct. 1995: A17.

Herszenhorn, David M. "New Marking System at Yale: A, B, C, D and X-Rated." *New York Times* 26 Jan. 2001: A21.

Hickman, Clayton. Review of *Guest House Paradiso. Film Review* Jan. 2000: 26.

Hill, John. *Sex, Class, and Realism: British Cinema 1956–1963.* London: BFI, 1986.

Hill, John, and Martin McLoone, eds. *Big Picture, Small Screen: The Relations between Film and Television.* Luton, UK: Libbey, 1995.

Hoberman, Jim. "A Pioneering Dialogue between Actress and Image." *New York Times* 22 Nov. 1998, sec. 21: 34.

"Hollywood Tragedies: The Price of Fame." *National Enquirer* 29 Feb. 2000: 21–51.

hooks, bell. *Reel to Real: Race, Sex, and Class at the Movies.* London: Routledge, 1996.

Hoptman, Laura. "Down to Zero: Yayoi Kusama and the European 'New Tendency.'" *Love Forever: Yayoi Kusama 1958–1968.* Ed. Thomas Frick. Los Angeles: Los Angeles County Museum of Art, 1998. 42–59.

Houston, Penelope. *Keepers of the Frame: The Film Archives.* London: BFI, 1994.

Huhtamo, Erkki. "Seeking Deeper Contact: Interactive Art as Metacommentary." *Convergence* 1.2 (Fall 1995): 81–104.

Hurst, Richard Maurice. *Republic Studios: Between Poverty Row and the Majors.* Metuchen, NJ: Scarecrow, 1979.

Hyams, Jay. *The Life and Times of the Western Movie.* New York: Gallery, 1983.

Israel, Lee. *Miss Tallulah Bankhead.* New York: Putnam, 1972.

Issari, Mohammad Ali. *Cinema in Iran, 1900–1979.* Metuchen, NJ: Scarecrow, 1989.

Jacobs, A. J. "The XXX Files." *Entertainment Weekly* 6 Aug. 1999: 20–25.

Jarvis, Everett Grant. *Final Curtain: Deaths of Noted Movie and Television Personalities.* Secaucus, NJ: Carol, 1996.

Juno, Andrea, and V. Vale, eds. *Angry Women.* San Francisco: Re/Search, 1991.

Kaiser, Charles. *The Gay Metropolis: 1940–1966.* San Diego: Harcourt, 1997.

Kakutani, Michiko. "Designer Nihilism." *New York Times Magazine* 24 Mar. 1996: 30+.

Kaplan, E. Ann. *Looking for the Other: Feminism, Film, and the Imperial Gaze.* New York: Routledge, 1997.

Katz, Jonathan Ned. *The Invention of Heterosexuality.* Foreword by Gore Vidal. New York: Plume, 1996.

Kauffman, Charlie. "Lawyer Blasts Defense of Marriage Amendment." *Daily Nebraskan* 2 Oct. 2001. 25 July 2001 <http://www.dailynebraskan.com/vnews/display.v/ART/2000/10/02/39d7fbb78>.

Kendall, Elizabeth. *The Runaway Bride: Hollywood Romantic Comedy of the 1930s.* New York: Anchor/Doubleday, 1990.

Kennedy, Burt. *Hollywood Trail Boss: Behind the Scenes of the Wild, Wild Western.* New York: Boulevard, 1997.

King, Stephen. *On Writing: A Memoir of the Craft.* New York: Scribner's, 2000.

Kirkham, Pat. "The Personal, the Professional, and the Partner(ship): The Husband/Wife Collaboration of Charles and Ray Eames." *Feminist Cultural Theory: Process and Production.* Ed. Beverly Skeggs. Manchester, UK: Manchester UP, 1995. 207–26.

Kirkham, Pat, and Janet Thumin, eds. *You Tarzan: Masculinity, Movies, and Men.* New York: St. Martin's, 1993.

Kirkpatrick, Sidney D. *A Cast of Killers.* New York: Dutton, 1986.

Kitses, Jim. *Horizons West: Anthony Mann, Budd Boetticher, Sam Peckinpah: Studies of Authorship within the Western.* Bloomington: Indiana UP, 1970.

Kobal, John. *People Will Talk.* New York: Knopf, 1985.

Kolbert, Elizabeth. "Pimps and Dragons." *New Yorker* 28 May 2001: 88–98.

Koning, Dirk. "No Sex, Please: Congress and the Courts Threaten Censorship of Cable Access, Internet." *Independent* 18.10 (Dec. 1995): 6+.

Koppang, Randy. "The Police State Is Now a Work of Art." *Paranoia* 8.1 (2001): 7–15.

Kotler, Steven. "Film Noir." *GQ* Mar. 2001: 256–61.

Kroker, Arthur, and Marilouise Kroker. *The Last Sex: Feminism and Outlaw Bodies.* New York: St. Martin's, 1993.

Laber, Emily. "Men Are from Quake, Women Are from Ultima." *New York Times* 11 Jan. 2000: D1+.

LaFerla, Ruth. "Perfect Model: Gorgeous, No Complaints, Made of Pixels." *New York Times* 7 May 2001: B8.

Laffey, Bruce. *Beatrice Lillie: The Funniest Woman in the World.* New York: Wynwood, 1989.

Lambert, Brian. "Producer Admits Reality in *Survivor* Is Faked." Pioneer Planet. 21 July 2001 <http://www.pioneerplanet.com/columnists/docs/LAMBERT/docs/035158.htm>.

Lambert, Gavin. *GWTW: The Making of* Gone with the Wind. Boston: Little, 1974.

Landay, Eileen. *Black Film Stars.* New York: Drake, 1973.

Landy, Marcia, ed. *Imitations of Life: A Reader on Film and Television Melodrama.* Detroit: Wayne State UP, 1991.

Langdon, Philip. *Orange Roofs, Golden Arches: The Architecture of American Chain Restaurants.* New York: Knopf, 1986.

Laqueur, Thomas. *Making Sex: Body and Gender from the Greeks to Freud.* Cambridge: Harvard UP, 1990.

Latham, Aaron. *Crazy Sundays.* New York: Viking, 1971.

Lawliss, Chuck. *Ghost Towns, Gold, & Gamblers.* New York: Gallery, 1985.

LeBlanc, Adrian Nicole. "The Outsiders." *New York Times Magazine* 22 Aug. 1999: 36–41.

Lenihan, John H. *Showdown: Confronting Modern America in the Western Film.* Urbana: U of Illinois P, 1980.

Lerner, Sharon. "Straightness 101: Christian Conservatives Take Their Antigay Campaign to the Schools." *Village Voice* 8 May 2001: 61–63.

Levy, Manuel. *George Cukor: Master of Elegance.* New York: Morrow, 1994.

Lewis, Jon. *The Road to Romance and Ruin: Teen Films and Youth Culture.* New York: Routledge, 1992.

Leyda, Jay, ed. *Voices of Film Experience: 1894 to the Present.* New York: Macmillan, 1977.

Leyda, Jay, and Charles Musser, eds. *Before Hollywood: Turn-of-the-Century Film from American Archives.* New York: American Federation of the Arts, 1986.

Linet, Beverly. *Ladd: The Life, the Legend, the Legacy of Alan Ladd.* New York: Berkeley, 1979.

Loos, Anita. *Fate Keeps on Happening.* London: Harrap, 1985.

Loulan, JoAnn. *Lesbian Passion.* San Francisco: Spinster, 1987.

Lovell, Mary S. *The Sound of Wings: The Life of Amelia Earhart.* New York: St. Martin's, 1989.

Lyons, Arthur. *Death on the Cheap: The Lost B Movies of Film Noir.* New York: Da Capo, 2000.

MacKinnon, James. "It's a Mad, Mad, Mad, Ad World." *Adbusters* 35 (2001): 84.

Madsen, Axel. *Forbidden Lovers: Hollywood's Greatest Secret—Female Stars Who Loved Other Women.* Secaucus, NJ: Carol, 1996.

Making of Guest House Paradiso, *The.* Ed Bye and Simon Burchell, Dir. Prod. Helen Parker. VVL Productions, in association with House Films, 1999.

Maltin, Leonard, ed. *Movie and Video Guide 1996.* New York: Plume, 1995.

Mamatas, Nick. "All Hands off the Keyboard!" *Village Voice* 31 Oct. 2000: 33–34.

Mandelbaum, Howard, and Eric Myers. *Forties Screen Style.* New York: St. Martin's, 1989.

Margulies, Ivone. *Nothing Happens: Chantal Akerman's Hyperrealist Everyday.* Durham: Duke UP, 1996.

Martin, Del, and Phyllis Lyon. *Lesbian/Woman.* San Francisco: Glide, 1972.

Matthews, Leonard. *History of Western Movies.* New York: Crescent, 1984.

Matthews, Tom D. *Censored.* London: Chatto, 1994.

Mavor, Carol. *Pleasures Taken: Performances of Sexuality and Loss in Victorian Photographs.* Durham: Duke UP, 1995.

Mayall, Rik. Web site. 3 June 2001 <http://www.wesjen.simplenet.com/rik/>; <http://www.wesjen.simplenet.com/rik/whosrik.htm>; <http://www.wesjen. simplenet.com/rik/projects.htm>; <http://www.wesjen.simplenet. com/rik/ riknews.htm>; and <http://www.wesjen.simplenet.com/rik/quotes.htm>.

Maynard, Richard A. *The American West on Film: Myth and Reality.* Rochelle Park, NJ: Hayden, 1974.

Mayne, Judith. "Uncovering the Female Body." *Before Hollywood: Turn-of-the-Century Film from American Archives.* Ed. Jay Leyda and Charles Musser. New York: American Federation of Arts, 1986. 63–67.

———. *Women at the Keyhole: Femininity and Women's Cinema.* Bloomington: Indiana UP, 1990.

McBride, Joseph. *Hawks on Hawks.* Berkeley: U of California P, 1982.

McCarthy, Todd, and Charles Flynn. *Kings of the Bs: Working within the Hollywood System.* New York: Dutton, 1975.

McCauley, Michael J. *Jim Thompson: Sleep with the Devil.* New York: Mysterious, 1991.

McClelland, Doug. *Forties Film Talk: Oral Histories of Hollywood.* Jefferson, NC: McFarland, 1992.

McDermott, Irene E., and Florence W. Nicholas. *Homemaking for Teen-agers.* Peoria, IL: Bennett, 1955.

McDonald, Myra. *Representing Women: Myths of Femininity in the Popular Media.* London: Arnold, 1992.

McDonald, Paul. *The Star System: Hollywood's Production of Popular Identities.* London: Wallflower, 2000.

McGilligan, Patrick. *George Cukor: A Double Life.* New York: St. Martin's, 1991.

Meyer, David N. *A Girl and a Gun: The Complete Guide to Film Noir on Video.* New York: Avon, 1998.

Miller, Neil. *Out of the Past: Gay and Lesbian History from 1869 to the Present.* New York: Vintage, 1995.

Mitchell, Lee Clark. *Westerns: Making the Man in Fiction and Film.* Chicago: U of Chicago P, 1996.

Mueller, Roswitha. *Valie Export: Fragments of the Imagination.* Bloomington: Indiana UP, 1994.

Mulvey, Laura. *Visual and Other Pleasures.* Bloomington: Indiana UP, 1989.

Murphy, Robert. *Sixties British Cinema.* London: BFI, 1992.

Murray, John A. *Cinema Southwest: An Illustrated Guide to the Movies and Their Locations.* Flagstaff, AZ: Northland, 2000.

Murray, Raymond. *Images in the Dark: An Encyclopedia of Gay and Lesbian Film and Video.* Philadelphia: TLA, 1994.

Musser, Charles. *Edison Motion Pictures, 1890–1900.* Washington, DC: Smithsonian, 1997.

Nachbar, Jack, ed. *Focus on the Western.* Englewood Cliffs, NJ: Prentice, 1974.

Nelson, Jim. "God Is on Line One." *GQ* Mar. 2001: 310–15+.

Nesheim, Eric, and Leif Nesheim. *Saucer Attack!* Los Angeles: Kitchen Sink, 1997.

New American Cinema Group. *Filmmakers' Cooperative Catalogue No. 4.* New York: New American Cinema Group, 1967.

Nichols, Bill. *Blurred Boundaries: Questions of Meaning in Contemporary Culture.* Bloomington: Indiana UP, 1994.

Null, Gary. *Black Hollywood: From 1910 to Today.* Secaucus, NJ: Citadel, 1993.

O'Brien, Geoffrey. *The Phantom Empire.* New York: Norton, 1993.

Old Tucson Studios. Hong Kong: Terrell, n.d.

Old Tucson Studios: Real to Reel. Dir. and screenwriter, Richard A. Rose. Videocassette. Tucson, AZ: Film Creations, 1997.

Owen, Gareth, with Brian Burford. *The Pinewood Story.* London: Reynolds, 2000.

Ozon, François. Presskit. *See the Sea.* New York: Zeitgeist, 1998.

Parish, James Robert. *Hollywood Character Actor.* New Rochelle, NY: Arlington, 1978.

Parisi, Paula. "Monster Job for Digital Domain." *Hollywood Reporter* 7–9 Oct. 1994: 1+.

Partners Task Force for Gay and Lesbian Couples. "'Defense of Marriage Act': Description and the Bill's Text." 25 July 2001 <http://www.buddybuddy. com/doma.html>.

Patrick, Robert. Foreword. *The Lavender Screen: The Gay and Lesbian Films: Their Stars, Makers, Characters, and Critics.* By Boze Hadleigh. New York: Citadel, 1993. 10–12.

Perry, Keith. Rev. of *Georges Méliès,* by Elizabeth Ezra. *6 Degrees.* 22 July 2001 <http://www.6degrees.co.uk/en/2/200008brgeorge.html>.

Peters, Margo. *The House of Barrymore.* New York: Knopf, 1960.

Pettigrew, Terence. *British Film Character Actors: Great Names and Memorable Moments.* London: David, 1982.

Phelan, Peggy. *Unmarked: The Politics of Performance.* London: Routledge, 1993.

Phelan, Peggy, and Jill Lane, eds. *The Ends of Performance.* New York: New York UP, 1998.

Plimpton! Showdown at Rio Lobo. By William Kronick and George Plimpton. With George Plimpton, John Wayne, Jennifer O'Neill, and Howard Hawks. Dir. and prod. William Kronick. ABC Television. 16 Dec. 1970.

Polito, Robert. *Savage Art: A Biography of Jim Thompson.* New York: Vintage, 1995.

"Privatopia." *Adbusters* 35 (2001): 29–34.

Quinlan, David. *The Illustrated Encyclopedia of Movie Character Actors.* New York: Harmony, 1985.

Rafferty, Terrence. "Invisible Man." *GQ* Mar. 2001: 239–44.

Rakoff, David. "Northern Light: Questions for Atom Egoyan." *New York Times Magazine* 12 Nov. 2000: 39.

Rawlence, Christopher. *The Missing Reel: The Untold Story of the Lost Inventor of Motion Pictures.* New York: Atheneum, 1990.

Redhead, Steve. *Unpopular Cultures: The Birth of Law and Popular Culture.* Manchester, UK: Manchester UP, 1995.

Renov, Michael. "*Leave Her to Heaven:* The Double Bind of the Post-War Woman." *Imitations of Life: A Reader on Film and Television Melodrama.* Ed. Marcia Landy. Detroit: Wayne State UP, 1991. 227–35.

Rich, Frank. "Naked Capitalists." *New York Times Magazine* 20 May 2001: 51–56+.

Richards, Dell. *Superstars: Twelve Lesbians Who Changed the World.* New York: Carroll, 1993.

Richards, Jeffrey, and Anthony Aldgate. *British Cinema and Society 1930–1970.* Totowa, NJ: Barnes, 1983.

Richtel, Matt. "Music and Movies Web Site in Bankruptcy-Law Filing." *New York Times* 14 Oct. 2000: B4.

Robinson, David. *Hollywood in the Twenties.* New York: Paperback/Coronet, 1970.

Roper, Jonathan. "The Heart of Multimedia: Interactivity or Experience?" *Convergence* 1.2 (Fall 1995): 23–28.

Ross, Robert. *The* Carry On *Companion.* London: Batsford, 1996.

———. *The Complete Sid James.* London: Reynolds, 2000.

Ross, Scott. "The Digital Domain." *Red Herring* Dec. 1993: 30–32.

Rowan, Geoffrey. "Seeing Is Disbelieving." *Globe and Mail: Report on Business* 15 Aug. 1994: B1+.

Russell, Dan. "The Racist Roots of the Drug War." *Paranoia* 8.1 (2001): 25–35.

Russo, Vito. *The Celluloid Closet: Homosexuality in the Movies.* Rev. ed. New York: Harper, 1987.

Sabin, Rob. "The Movies' Digital Future Is in Sight and It Works." *New York Times* 26 Nov. 2000, sec. 2: 1+.

Safire, William. "On Language: Rollout; The Film, Not the Barrel." *New York Times Magazine* 12 Nov. 2000: 42+.

Schimmel, Paul, ed. *Out of Actions: Between Performance and the Object, 1949–1979.* New York: Thames, 1998.

Schwartz, Charles. *Cole Porter: A Biography.* New York: Dial, 1977.

Seabrook, John. *Nobrow: The Culture of Marketing—The Marketing of Culture.* New York: Knopf, 2000.

Sedgwick, Eve Kosofsky. *Epistemology of the Closet.* Berkeley: U of California P, 1990.

Seltzer, Mark. *Bodies and Machines.* New York: Routledge, 1992.

Senn, Brian. *Drums of Terror: Voodoo in the Cinema.* Baltimore: Midnight Marquee, 1998.

Server, Lee. *Robert Mitchum: "Baby, I Don't Care."* New York: St. Martin's, 2001.

Seymour, Gene. "We've Gotta Have It: Black Filmmakers Seize the Moment." *Nation* 272.13 (2 Apr. 2001): 12–17.

Shaviro, Stephen. *The Cinematic Body.* Minneapolis: U of Minnesota P, 1993.

Shohat, Ella. "Gender and Culture of Empire: Toward a Feminist Ethnography of the Cinema." *Visions of the East: Orientalism in Film.* Ed. Matthew Bernstein and Gaylyn Studlar. New Brunswick, NJ: Rutgers UP, 1997. 19–66.

Signorile, Michelangelo. *Queer in America.* New York: Random, 1993.

Silents Majority. Web site. 5 July 2001 <http://www.mdle.com/ClassicFilms/SpecialFeature/fool.htm>.

Silver, Alain, and James Ursini. *The Vampire Film: From* Nosferatu *to* Bram Stoker's Dracula. Rev. ed. New York: Limelight, 1993.

Sinclair, Iain. *Crash.* London: BFI, 1999.

Skeggs, Beverly, ed. *Feminist Cultural Theory: Process and Production.* Manchester, UK: Manchester UP, 1995.

Slane, Andrea. *A Not So Foreign Affair: Fascism, Sexuality, and the Cultural Rhetoric of American Democracy.* Durham: Duke UP, 2001.

Slide, Anthony. *Early Women Directors.* S. Brunswick, NJ: Barnes, 1977.

Smiley, Jane. "The Dream Factory: Me and My Product." *New York Times Magazine* 12 Nov. 2000: 35–36.

Smith, Judith E. "The Marrying Kind: Working-Class Courtship and Marriage in 1950s Hollywood." *Multiple Voices in Feminist Film Criticism.* Ed. Diane Carson, Linda Dittmar, and Janice R. Welsch. Minneapolis: U of Minnesota P, 1994. 226–42.

Sontag, Susan. "The Decay of Cinema." *New York Times Magazine* 25 Feb. 1996: 60–61.

Specter, Michael. "The Doomsday Click." *New Yorker* 28 May 2001: 101–07.

Sperber, A. M., and Eric Lax. *Bogart.* New York: Morrow, 1997.

Spigel, Lynn. *Welcome to the Dreamhouse: Popular Media and Postwar Suburbs.* Durham: Duke UP, 2001.

Spoto, Donald. *Blue Angel: The Life of Marlene Dietrich.* New York: Doubleday, 1992.

Stacey, Jackie. "The Lost Audience: Methodology, Cinema History, and Feminist Film Criticism." *Feminist Culture Theory: Process and Production.* Ed. Beverly Skeggs. Manchester, UK: Manchester UP, 1995. 97–118.

Staiger, Janet. *Bad Women: Regulating Sexuality in Early American Cinema.* Minneapolis: U of Minnesota P, 1995.

Stam, Robert, Robert Burgoyne, and Sandy Flitterman-Lewis. *New Vocabularies in Film Semiotics.* London: Routledge, 1992.

Straayer, Chris. *Deviant Eyes, Deviant Bodies: Sexual Re-Orientations in Film and Video.* New York: Columbia UP, 1996.

"Straight." *The American Heritage College Dictionary.* 3rd ed. New York: Houghton Mifflin, 1993.

Street, Sarah. *British National Cinema.* London: Routledge, 1997.

Suárez, Juan, and Millicent Manglis. "Cinema, Gender, and the Topography of Enigmas: A Conversation with Laura Mulvey." *Cinefocus* 3 (1995): 2–8.

Suleiman, Susan Rubin. *Risking Who One Is: Encounters with Contemporary Art and Literature.* Cambridge: Harvard UP, 1994.

Swimme, Brian. "The Religion of the Ad." *Sun* 305 (2001): 16–19.

Talbot, Margaret. "Nip, Tuck, and Frequent-Flier Miles." *New York Times Magazine* 6 May 2001: 86–90.

Tasker, Yvonne. *Working Girls: Gender and Sexuality in Popular Cinema.* London: Routledge, 1998.

Taylor, Craig. "Heir of the Dogma: Questions for Ernest Adams." *New York Times Magazine* 15 Apr. 2001: 13.

Thomas, Bob. *Joan Crawford: A Biography.* New York: Simon, 1978.

Thomas, Tony, and Aubrey Solomon. *The Films of 20th Century Fox: A Pictorial History.* Secaucus, NJ: Citadel, 1985.

Thompson, Anne. "The George Lucas Interview." *Premiere* May 1999: 68–77.

Todorov, Tzvetan. *The Morals of History.* Trans. Alyson Waters. Minneapolis: U of Minnesota P, 1995.

Toulet, Emmanuelle. *Birth of the Motion Picture.* Trans. Susan Emanuel. New York: Abrams, 1995.

Vaughn, Robert. *Only Victims: A Study of Show Business Blacklisting.* New York: Putnam's, 1972.

Veblen, Thorstein. *The Theory of the Leisure Class.* New York: Dover, 1994.

Vermont Defense of Marriage PAC. "Our Mission." 25 July 2001 <http://www. vtdompac.com/docs/our_mission.htm>.

Walker, Janet. "Hollywood, Freud, and the Representation of Women: Regulation and Contradiction, 1945–Early 60s." *Home Is Where the Heart Is: Studies in Melodrama and the Women's Film.* Ed. Christine Gledhill. London: BFI, 1987. 197–214.

Wallace, Irving, Amy Wallace, David Wallechinsky, and Sylvia Wallace. *The Intimate Sex Lives of Famous People.* New York: Delacorte, 1981.

Walsh, Raoul. *Each Man in His Own Time: The Life Story of a Director.* New York: Farrar, 1974.

Warren, Patricia. *British Film Studios: An Illustrated History.* London: Batsford, 1995.

Weldon, Michael. *The Psychotronic Encyclopedia of Film.* New York: Ballantine, 1983.

Wells, Paul. *The Horror Genre: From* Beelzebub *to* Blair Witch. London: Wallflower, 2000.

White, Patricia. *Uninvited: Classical Hollywood Cinema and Lesbian Representability.* Bloomington: Indiana UP, 1999.

Wiegman, Robyn. *American Anatomies: Theorizing Race and Gender.* Durham: Duke UP, 1995.

Williams, Kenneth. *Just Williams—An Autobiography.* London: Dent, 1985.

———. *The Kenneth Williams Diaries.* Ed. Russell Davies. London: HarperCollins, 1993.

———. *The Kenneth Williams Letters.* Ed. Russell Davies. London: HarperCollins, 1994.

Williams, Raymond. "Argument: Text and Performance." *The Twentieth Century Performance Reader.* Ed. Michael Huxley and Noel Witts. London: Routledge, 1996. 369–83.

Wills, Claire. "*Bottom* Star Directs Himself and Rik Mayall in *Guest House Paradiso.*" *Flicks* (Nov. 1999); Adrian Edmondson Web Site.

Windsor, Barbara. *Barbara—The Laughter and Tears of a Cockney Sparrow.* London: Century, 1990.

Wolgamott, Kent L. "Fiction Writer Jim Thompson Got His Start at NU in Lincoln." *Lincoln Journal* 28 Feb. 1991: 15.

Wood, John, ed. *The Virtual Embodied: Presence/Practice/Technology.* London: Routledge, 1998.

Wright, Will. *Six Guns and Society: A Structural Study of the Western.* Berkeley: U of California P, 1975.

Zavarzadeh, Mas'ud. *Seeing Films Politically.* Albany: State U of New York P, 1991.

ABOUT THE AUTHOR

Wheeler Winston Dixon is the James Ryan Endowed Professor of Film Studies, Chairperson of the Film Studies Program, Professor of English at the University of Nebraska, Lincoln; series editor for the State University of New York Press Cultural Studies in Cinema/Video; and the Editor in Chief, with Gwendolyn Audrey Foster, of the *Quarterly Review of Film and Video*.

INDEX